BEYOND SUPER WOMAN

Anxiety, strength and the spaces in-between

BEYOND SUPER WOMAN

CINDY MOUSSI

Copyright © 2018 Cindy Moussi

All rights reserved. No part of this publication may be reproduced, stored in a retrieval system, or transmitted in any form or by any means without the prior written permission of the publisher, nor be otherwise circulated in any form of binding or cover other than that in which it is published and without a similar condition being imposed on the subsequent purchaser.

Publisher: 135 PRESS, Melbourne Victoria Australia

Author Email: cindy@cindymoussi.com

ISBN-13: 978-0-6482408-0-8

A catalogue record for this book is available from
the National Library of Australia.

Cover photography: Verve Photography
Cover design & interior formatting: Mark Thomas / Coverness.com

Disclaimer

All care has been taken in the preparation of the information herein, but no responsibility can be accepted by the publisher or author for any damages resulting from the misinterpretation of this work. The advice given in this book is based on the experience of the individuals. Professionals should be consulted for individual problems. The author and publisher shall not be responsible for any person with regard to any loss or damage caused directly or indirectly by the information in this book.

TABLE OF CONTENTS

About The Author i

Dedication iii

Fear Will Take You Down 1

BIRTH.. 5

GROWING UP 21

DEFINED... 89

HIGH OCTANE... 147

KRYPTONITE... 219

DEATH.. 261

TRANSFORMED 341

Resources 365

Special Thanks 369

ABOUT THE AUTHOR

Born in Beirut in 1970, Cindy Moussi has lived her life between Lebanon and Australia. From a childhood surrounded by her birth country's many vicious wars, to her teenage years in Australia, to almost two decades advancing in the corporate world, Cindy has lately yearned to sort out her identity and get back to her roots.

After struggling with anxiety, she became passionate about bringing awareness to anxiety and how to heal from it. She's a mother, a lover of travel, and in addition to writing, Cindy holds an accounting degree, a Doctorate of Philosophy, and is also a professionally certified executive coach.

She's currently taking the time to reconnect with herself, hike the mountains of Lebanon, and work on her next project.

Beyond Superwoman is her first book.

DEDICATION

To my son, Alexander, my mother, Leila, and all anxiety sufferers.

FEAR WILL TAKE YOU DOWN

I wake up with the same terror, my fear leading the way. I feel like everything is going to come crashing down on me. I find myself in a void with no purpose to propel me forward. Instead, this void gives space to my long ignored exhaustion and repressed pain. It dredges up old memories of fear and shame that have manifested themselves in ways I never imagined possible. Physical pain. Unrelenting and crippling anxiety. Despair so deep, my life no longer feels like it is worth living. I see no way out of this darkness.

I try everything: meditation, mindfulness, presence, being guided by God, going to the gym to get fit, praying, reading… I am desperate for answers, and I'm exhausted by all my trying. I'm told to just *be* with the feelings. I try. But they are too painful. How can feeling these feelings be a good thing, especially when I wake up shaking with terror every day? Fear now has a permanent grip on me. It is at its worse in the morning. I have no appetite and am losing weight rapidly. I have to force myself to eat in spite of the constant feeling of being punched in the gut; this is where my dread lodges itself.

I wake up each day and say to myself, *Cindy, just get out of bed. You know sleeping all day will make it worse. Just get up. Don't go down the tunnel. Now, make your bed. Just make your bed. Go make a cup of tea. Sit down and know that all there is to do is drink your cup of tea. Now, go have a shower. Go to the gym. Go to the gym. Just go. You don't have to feel like it.*

This is the level of self-talk that is keeping me safe.

Everything feels so hard. Feeding myself, answering emails, catching up with friends. I don't feel like it. It is too exhausting to have to make conversation. It is physically painful to even talk, let alone listen. However, the worse I feel, the more Buddha-like I appear to others. Peaceful, calm, and serene. No one can tell by looking at me how much pain I am in. I begin to close off from the world as I shift from shame to despondency.

I want a formula. I want answers. Someone to save me from this hell I'm starting to think I'll never climb out of. What I yearn for during these darkest days is to climb back into my mother's womb. To be held. To be rocked. But Mum is dealing with my dying father and is unable to give me these things. Where else does one go with their excruciating pain? So few people can provide that womb for us. And as I reckon with my darkness, I come to realise that only *I* can provide that womb for myself. But my faith in my ability is waning.

I can live with the anxiety, even the depression, but when I am hit with unrelenting terror attacks, I feel I cannot cope any longer. If this is what every day is going to be like, I want out—I'm not a great martyr. "What is the point of anything?" becomes my daily inquiry.

Death starts to feel like the only answer. The only respite from the agony and constant terror.

But I can't give up.

I slowly learn that I have to surrender my old ways of

searching for answers outside of myself and begin to listen for the answers in an entirely new way.

Eventually, I find the courage to go back and face my past with honesty and compassion. This requires a willingness to dare to listen to my deeper knowing and trust it. I also begin to learn that my pain is not just about me. It goes deeper than that. It has family roots, and history, and those roots began as I did—in Lebanon.

BIRTH

I am child
I am open
I am love

...if a person grows up in a time of war or in a family and community that is suffering, that person may be full of despair and fear...Making peace with your ancestors takes some practice, but it is important to reconcile with them if you are to settle the fear within yourself...

— Thich Nhat Hanh

The Ottoman Empire should be cleaned up of the Armenians and the Lebanese. We have destroyed the former by the sword, we shall destroy the latter through starvation.

— Ismail Enver

HAIRDOS, NUNS, AND THE PARIS OF THE MIDDLE EAST

My mum, Leila, was the youngest of four children born in Beirut, Lebanon. Beirut was in its prime. This was the 1950s, and it was the Paris of the Middle East. Beirut in those days was quite remarkable. Martyr's Square (then known as *Sahat al-Burj*) was lively and full of energy, a place of coffee houses, cinemas, fashion, and elegance. A tad different from what it was like when I was growing up there in the '70s and '80s!

It fascinated me when Mum would share stories of her life. In that Middle Eastern, middle-class kind of way, Mum's family was considered well-to-do. They lived a comfortable life of days now long past. A life that was simple, yet saturated with sophistication.

Mum often shared the story of her older sister having a seamstress come to sew her gowns for special occasions. As it was told, they lived a very romantic existence, indeed. While the four children did share one bedroom, they also had a live-in maid. There was an ongoing joke that my mother used to get the maid to carry a box of tissues around, so if she needed one it would always be on hand.

Because she was the youngest, Mum was adored and spoilt

by her father. He'd let her climb up onto his shoulders while he was drinking his morning coffee, which drove my grandmother crazy. And when she would dig into his pockets to get all the change she could hold, he delighted in letting her keep it. This obviously wasn't something that went unnoticed by her siblings, which often made her a target for being relentlessly teased.

Mum had two sisters and a brother. They all went to boarding school in Beirut during the winters when my grandmother, who suffered from asthma, needed to go to Egypt where the air was warmer and drier. Mum, with her two sisters, went to a French school, St. Joseph de L'apparition, which was run by Lebanese and European nuns. It was one of the best Catholic schools in Beirut, and it attracted all walks of life and religions. Local children, diplomats' children, Muslim children, Palestinian children, as well as African expatriates who sent their children back home to get a Lebanese education. According to my mum, these nuns were not the loving kind. Mum regularly had her hair put under the tap to douse her latest hairdo in water. This situation escalated one day when she was found fixing her hair in the reflection of a window. One of the Lebanese nuns came over, and with a pair of scissors, cut off all of Mum's hair. Such vanity was not to be tolerated. Needless to say, Mum was not such a big fan of the the nuns after that. And before long, she lost interest in her academic life.

By the age of sixteen, she took up a secretarial course at the YMCA. She loved fashion, and by dropping a few subjects, she was able to save enough money to fund her love of clothes and shopping. All hell broke loose when her mother found out. To add insult to injury, she fell in love with the 'wrong' boy. To get her away from him, she was lured into spending at least one year in Australia to see how she liked it. If she didn't, she was told she could return. But this would mean leaving her father!

My grandfather, Toufic, was born in Aleppo, Syria. His father, my great-grandfather, Nasri, an extremely wealthy man, had fled to Syria from Turkey to escape the Armenian and Christian genocide which resulted in over 1.5 million deaths. It was an era of massacres, rape, and robbery. He had to leave everything behind to save his family.

My grandfather owned a traditional Lebanese mezza house in Beirut. It was quite the establishment, popular for its traditional Lebanese appetisers and known for serving some of the best *arak,* an anise-flavored aperitif, you could find. To the disappointment of his patrons, he would close the restaurant for the three months of summer, and the entire family would go and stay in the mountains, a common luxury of the times.

My grandfather still had deeds to his father's property in Turkey. However it would not have been safe for him to return there to claim this land. Even though he'd been born after the massacres in Turkey, he lived through the aftermath of his own father having to leave it all behind, which had quite an impact on him. So, despite making a lot of money from his successful little business, he refused to invest in material things. His family was his investment, he would say. "I have four children. They are my four buildings."

Mum was seventeen when she left her beloved Beirut to join her siblings in Australia. As it turned out, she was also leaving the father she adored at a time when he was getting quite sick.

Little did she know it would be the last time she would see him. It was a seventeen-day boat trip, and when she finally arrived in Australia, it was a complete culture shock for my young, sophisticated mother. She went from the Paris of the Middle East to rural Victoria in the blink of an eye. "Who paints their house blue and pink?" Mum would often share when referring to these times. Eventually, she lived with her brother, Nasri, and her cousin, Maroun, above the café they both owned in Colac.

She worked hard in their café. Her day would start at nine in the morning and often finish at two in the morning. All the while, she could barely understand the Australian accent. It was a miserable experience for her, feeling completely alone and so very far away from her familiar and beautiful life in Beirut. Those feelings only intensified when she soon received the news that her father had died. "I felt like an orphan," she would share. She had adored him, and now he—along with her old life—was gone.

COUSINS, CAFÉS, AND MARRIAGE

Where Mum's family was poised with the air of old-Lebanese sophistication, Dad's family might be considered more the 'peasant' relatives, so to speak. Oh, but the fun we had with Dad's side of the family! There were nine children all together—six brothers and three sisters. They grew up in a one-room house settled amongst banana and orange groves on the coast of the Mediterranean Sea, taking baths in the village water channel that passed in front of the house. They grew up close to the land and the sea.

My dad, Maroun, was a simple man. He was Mum's first cousin. He arrived in Australia four years before my mother, at the age of sixteen, with the equivalent of two dollars in his pocket. When Dad first arrived in Australia, he worked for his eldest brother, Antoine, in his café in Colac, 150 kilometres south-west of the state capital, Melbourne. Dad always shared stories about my uncle ruthlessly working him and his other brothers seven days a week, only getting an occasional afternoon off to go see a movie. Despite being bitter about those days, he also knew the responsibility instilled in Antoine at an early age.

Antoine was only eleven when he went to Beirut to work,

and though it was in some of the classiest hotels in the city, learning the trade at a high level of sophistication, imagine the responsibility of having to feed your parents and eight siblings. He was a bit hardened by his life. Hard work was his only beat. Now, just like his brother Antoine did, Dad worked and sent money home to educate his younger siblings.

Before long the Moussi brothers, as they were known, became legend in Colac. Despite all the hard work, they had a sense of humour, and there was something about the level of real Lebanese hospitality they would give. Cafés became their thing. Given their work ethic and love of people, they soon cashed in.

My grandfather on Dad's side, Naamtallah, was often sick. He was part-farmer, part-fisherman. A soft and gentle man with blond hair and kind blue eyes. Naamtallah's father, my great-grandfather, Moussi, was a wealthy boat-owning man who sailed the seas as a trader. During World War I, he got trapped outside Lebanon only to return years later a rich man, loaded with gold and diamonds. Upon his return, he was welcomed by a family that had barely survived the Great Famine of 1915-1918, a time when 200,000 people—half the population of Lebanon—were decimated from starvation.

My grandmother on Dad's side was the polar-opposite of her sister, who was my Mum's mother. That's right, my grandmothers, my *tetas*, were sisters. Where my grandmother on Mum's side, Edma, could be considered 'Queen of Sophistication,' Dad's mum, Olga, was more like 'Queen of the Village.' Teta Edma was one of the first women in Lebanon to drive a car in her day, sacking her driver to assert her independence and literally getting into the driver's seat. Whereas Teta Olga was the orbit around which the village revolved.

When I used to stay with Teta Olga in Lebanon, I would wake early to the sound of the village women gathered in her dining room. At five in the morning! This was known as the *soubheyyeh*, a ritual that was the fabric of village life in Lebanon. While my teta ironed sheets and undies, the ladies caught up on current village affairs and gossip. On the odd occasion I managed to sleep until seven, Teta Olga would storm into my bedroom, whip off my doona, and say, "Get up, it's noon." Regardless, I loved the feeling of this authentic village existence and would often wake to join the women.

The money Teta Olga's children sent home to her from Australia would quickly slip through her fingers because she used it to help others she believed to be less fortunate. One of my uncles bought her an almost endless supply of hand-made Lebanese soap. It was not uncommon to stock up in this way. However, by the time that uncle returned a year later, it was all gone. According to my grandmother, "Others were in need." This wasn't very easy for her children, as they truly worked their lives away in Australia. Despite my grandmother's detached ways of dealing with money, making some of my uncles feel quietly resentful, they never stopped sending their hard-earned money home to Lebanon. She was their mother after all, and it was their job to look after her. Such was their culture.

*

Mum was unhappy in this isolated country life. It was my father she would turn to for comfort. Over time, comfort turned into more. My mum's mother, Teta Edma, disapproved of this relationship. The tide had turned, and now my grandmother was trying to encourage my mum to return to Lebanon to get her away from Dad. She failed, and eventually my parents eloped. Mum was only nineteen and Dad was twenty-four. But as soon as they were married, Teta Edma dropped her disapproval as if overnight—that annoying and hypocritical Lebanese trait. But city sophisticate and earthy villager were not a match made in heaven.

BIRTH, BREATH, AND RAS BEIRUT

"Maroun, if I fall pregnant again, I'm going to Lebanon to have the baby. I simply can't cope with another child." True to Mum's word I was born in Beirut, Lebanon on the twenty-sixth of November in 1970. My beginning wasn't easy—I was born black and blue with the umbilical cord wrapped around my neck. I wasn't breathing, and the doctor had to hold me upside down and smack me on the bottom to get me to take my first breath. My older brother was just two, and my sister barely one, when Mum became pregnant for the third time. Having three children under the age of three would be a lot for anyone, but especially for Mum, who was just twenty-three.

Who could blame her for wanting to return to Lebanon for the support she desperately needed? Not to mention this was quite normal in our culture. So, this is how my affinity with Lebanon began.

I've always held a great sense of pride from being born in Beirut. My older siblings were born in Australia; my brother in Colac, and my sister in Geelong, a larger town just southwest of Melbourne. For some reason, being born in Lebanon gave me a certain sense of pride. I had quite the air of superiority when

I used to explain to people that not only was I born in Beirut, but I was born in Ras Beirut. This translates into "The Head of Beirut," which was a small piece of Lebanon that jetted out into the Mediterranean Sea. While that kind of arrogance seems a bit silly these days, back then it made me feel very important.

When I was born, my father was still in Australia. So, it was by letter that he informed my mum that he wished to name me after his mother, Olga! It just so happened to be that my mum was with my dad's mum when the letter was read out loud. Mum obviously felt obligated to give me my grandmother's name, given the culture. She got around this obligation by choosing a more French sounding middle name—Cynthia. Olga Cynthia Moussi it was. From then on, however, Mum called me Cindy. Not once have I ever heard my mother call me Olga or Cynthia, not even when I was in trouble.

My mother, my siblings, and I were back in Australia before my first birthday. We lived in a beautiful home in Geelong that overlooked the Barwon River. The décor in my first childhood home exemplified my mum's style perfectly, chic and in fashion. Her upbringing in Beirut had left a strong imprint on her, and it revealed itself in the way she showcased her home. Impeccable, to say the least. While Mum absorbed herself in her home and motherhood, Dad absorbed himself in his work.

ARABIC, LEMON TREES, AND TERMS OF ENDEARMENT

Growing up in Australia, I listened to Arabic in a very literal way. Things that were normal for a Lebanese mother to mutter when frustrated went straight to the heart, leaving me feeling traumatised. When Mum said things like, "Goddamn the hour I had children in it," or, "I'm going to beat you until something comes out of the floor and beats you," I took them very literally. There were also the times when, "I'm going to slap you and make you spit blood," or, "I'll slap you and remove your face," were taken by me to be things that were indeed going to happen. How was I supposed to know they were simply Lebanese parenting threats?

Later in life, my cousins and I would lovingly joke about how bad these sayings were. Could we ever imagine speaking to our children this way? The thing is, when we compared notes with native Lebanese people who weren't raised in Australia, they couldn't comprehend what was so terrible. They didn't hear these Arabic phrases so literally and found it strange we could ever be so traumatised by them. Still, they left me feeling quite unsettled, not to mention altogether unloved.

Then of course, there was the dreaded 'lemon tree stick' on

top of every good Lebanese relative's refrigerator. It was called the *adeeb* and was equivalent to the strap. This was yet another topic for the cousins to joke about when we got older. Humour really was our therapy. We would laugh about how all our parents had an *adeeb*, and how they would test the 'whipping' factor when choosing a branch that would make a good strap. And while I can't even remember ever being hit with the *adeeb* that lived on top of our own refrigerator, I do know I lived in terror of it ever being used.

My sister once told me her own lemon tree story. Mum had told her to go outside and choose her own whip. So my sister, who didn't seem to hold the same fear of Mum as I did, went outside and picked out a little twig. She came back inside and told my mother that it was all she could find. Mum just laughed. As I'm sure my sister did, too. I would have given anything to have my sister's sense of humour.

While Arabic has some of the most traumatising phrases I've ever heard, it also has the most loving and moving terms of endearment. Usually these terms are just one word, but each contains a beautiful phrase when translated into English.

Hayeteh: You are my life.

Ya'aouneh: You are my eyes.

Ya'albeh: You are my heart.

Ya Rouhe: You are my spirit/soul.

Toukoubrineh: May you live longer than me and be the person that buries me.

Kind of difficult to translate that one!

I remember the first time a Lebanese man said *hayeteh* to me. I thought I'd died and gone to heaven. In this way, Arabic could literally melt my heart. For this man, *hayeteh* could have been the same as sweetheart, but add a little eye gaze in there, and I was gone!

I'm not sure why my parents would use these terms of endearment more with other people than with their own children. Perhaps some protective mechanism. Regardless, I yearned for more verbal affection.

But while I was convinced I was not loved by my parents, my mum was bending over backwards reading every psychology book that existed on how to better raise her children, and my dad was slaving his life away trying to provide us with a better life than his. Unfortunately, as is the case with many families, my parents' own childhood pain and trauma—of scarcity for my father and fear of abandonment for my mother —often spilt over and cut like a knife. Which was something that often made it difficult to feel their unconditional love.

Along with the feeling of being unloved, came the contradiction of being Mum's confidante. Mum had a trust in me that built my self-esteem in ways I could only see later in life. But despite the building of my self-esteem, at times it also overloaded me as a young girl and woman. I often felt like my mum's little counsellor, knowing all about their money issues and relationship problems.

Nothing in our home was sacred. Nothing was left unsaid. Secrets? We had none. While this is great on one hand, there's a level of appropriateness that was far overlooked. But who was there to teach my parents the meaning of appropriateness? Boundaries? These were foreign concepts to Mum and Dad. There was simply little understanding of the concept of 'oversharing.'

GROWING UP

I am Lebanese
I am Australian
I am confused

We leave something of ourselves behind when we leave a place, we stay there, even though we go away. And there are things in us that we can find again only by going back there.
— Pascal Mercier

Don't be ashamed of reliving your childhood, Ox, because all of us must do it now and then to maintain our sanity.
— Barry Hughart

I'M BORED...
LET'S GET OUT OF HERE

Something felt like it was missing in this perfect, stable life of abundance. Then suddenly, things didn't feel so stable anymore. It was as if overnight, Mum and Dad sold our gorgeous home and almost everything else they owned. Life in Australia, as we knew it, was about to change. On a whim, it seemed, Dad bought an industrial dry-cleaning business in Lebanon. And not just any dry-cleaning business. Dad bought the largest industrial dry cleaning business in the Middle East. Left behind was a successful bakery called Tim's Pies and Kay's Cakes, a great business partner, and a life of reliable financial abundance.

When my parents were starting out, they didn't think in terms of a career. It was more about survival and making money. However, by the time Mum and Dad sold everything and bought the dry-cleaning business, the game of survival had been over for some time. I wonder if that left Mum and Dad a bit lost. Bored, perhaps. Maybe it was suburban life that lacked any life force. Perhaps killing it. It certainly killed mine when I attempted it many years later.

Unbeknownst to my father at the time, who had sold

everything and purchased the dry-cleaning business, he was soon to be challenged on many different levels. For one, he had no experience whatsoever in the dry-cleaning industry. Secondly, the war in Lebanon was not even close to being over, even though my parents had heard news stating it was.

I admire the adventurous side of Mum and Dad. If nothing else, they had guts. When I asked Mum many years later what possessed them to make such a move, she said they wanted to be home with their people. The allure of a peaceful Lebanon filled them with the courage to completely uproot themselves, their three children, and their comfortably abundant life. And though they were hopeful for the future in front of them, sadly, the war wasn't over yet. It was 1977, and a peaceful invasion led by the Syrians had temporarily stabilised the country…but the peace side of the invasion didn't last for long.

SHAKY FOUNDATIONS: LEBANON'S POLITICAL HISTORY

The Lebanese achieved their independence from the French in 1941, but only in principle, given the French continued to impose their authority. In 1943, after much resistance by the French, Lebanon formed its first democratic government and the foundations of the State were announced: the President was to be a Maronite Christian, the Prime Minister, a Sunni Muslim, and the Speaker of the Chamber of Deputies, a Shia Muslim. And on January 1, 1944, France agreed to transfer power to the Lebanese government.

Initially, the establishment of the government was seen as a big step forward. However, as time passed, the religious makeup of the population changed, and resentment set in with the various religious factions. The Muslims resented the Christians for having the upper hand, given that they, the Christians, were becoming the minority. The Shia resented the Sunnis because they had even less power than the Sunnis did. This lack of fair religious representation would eventually lead to many problems and the deaths of thousands.

Around this time, neighbouring Palestine had its own fair share of internal turmoil brewing. There was a huge influx of Jews fleeing Germany and seeking to set up a Jewish homeland in Palestine. This movement was called Zionism. Initially, the U.S. wanted to set limits on Jewish immigration to Palestine and supported the creation of provinces rather than states. However, they eventually decided to support the formation of the State of Israel, though the British, who held a colonial mandate for Palestine, were not too happy about that. They opposed both the creation of a Jewish state and an Arab state in Palestine, as well as unlimited immigration of Jewish refugees to the region. They wanted to preserve good relations with the Arabs, which they saw as the only way to protect their vital political and economic interests in Palestine.

Conflict began to escalate in the region, and its target was the newly formed Jewish State, Israel. As the conflict escalated in Palestine, Palestinian refugees began arriving in Lebanon in 1948. No one expected the situation to go on for as long as it did.

PEACEKEEPING, SUNBAKING, AND WORLD CLASS HOSPITALITY

By 1958, a civil war had erupted in Lebanon. Syria and Egypt were angling to form a United Arab Republic, and they wanted Lebanon to be part of it. The Lebanese Muslims and Druze were all for the joining, however, the Christians did not want to play ball.

This brought about great civil unrest, claiming between two and four thousand lives. To add fuel to the fire, on July 14, 1958 a revolution overthrew the Hashemite monarchy in Iraq. The entire royal family was killed. The revolutionaries were inspired by the vision of an Arab State as well as being fed up with Western interference, especially by the British. There were threats that the Lebanese, pro-Western Chamoun family would be next. Chamoun, the Lebanese president, immediately summoned the ambassadors of the United States, Britain, and France, requesting assistance.

Despite the civil war resulting in significant loss of life, it was short lived. When five thousand United States Marines landed on the shores of Lebanon, they were greeted by sunbathers and swimmers. Their role? Support the Lebanese government against foreign invasion. This intervention was regarded by many as an overreaction and perhaps a 'comic opera,' as some have referred to it. Most Marines have very fond memories of 'saving the day' during their post in Lebanon. Gorgeous women, great beaches, parties, real hospitality. Many were sad to leave.

A MASSACRE HERE, A MASSACRE THERE. PASS ME THE ARAK

The tension between the Arab States and the State of Israel continued to escalate over the years, culminating in the Arab-Israeli Six-Day War in 1967. Although Lebanon did not play an active role in this war, it was involved by virtue of the Palestinians using Lebanon as a base for attacks on Israel. The Palestinian Liberation Organisation (the PLO) was taking a hold in Lebanon. By the 1970s, conflict between the Lebanese Christian and Muslim groups flared up. Christian groups opposed the presence of armed PLO members in Lebanon, but Muslim groups supported it. Also, the country's Muslim population had grown, justifying their demands for more power in the government. The PLO supported the Muslims in these demands. The Christians opposed Muslim demands for increased power in the government and resented the alliance between the Muslims and the PLO.

Conflict intensified in 1975 after a church was fired upon in East Beirut, killing four people, including two Phalangists (members of a Maronite political party). The Palestinians were blamed for the attack. In retaliation, thirty Palestinians were killed by a Gemayel (head of the Phalangist Party)-led group of Phalangists.

I grew up constantly hearing about this massacre and many others. These massacres would continue as the civil war went from shocking, to life as usual. They were so traumatising that the need to share, discuss, process, understand, agree, disagree, blame, justify, feel glee, shame, grief, despair, victory, humiliation, and defeat was never-ending. How could it not be? With two degrees of separation in Lebanon, everyone was touched by each death. I was only five years old when this particular massacre occurred and still not living in Lebanon. However, this story, like many others, was more like legend, to be told and retold. This was one of the many massacres that was etched in the dark recesses of my mind. I could not make sense of these stories. I knew the people that were part of these political parties, and they were ordinary people with families. They did not evoke fear in those around them. They went to church, funerals, weddings, christenings. They lent a helping hand, right there when you needed them.

Eventually, a brutal civil war broke out between the Christians and the Muslim-PLO alliance. Beirut was split up into Christian Beirut and Muslim Beirut. The fighting killed tens of thousands of people and caused widespread property damage. More massacres ensued, deepening the hatred and entrenching a never-ending cycle of revenge. Now who was to blame—the Jews for taking over Israel, the Palestinians who fought their battles out of Lebanon, the Muslims, the Christians, the French, the Brits, the U.S.? Blame was the currency of the time. But never fear, Syria was near!

ILLUSIONS OF PEACE

In 1976, the Syrians came to the rescue upon the request of the then President Suleiman Frangieh. Christian groups supported this. The aim was to curb the Palestinians. Strangely, this put Syria on the side of Israel. This shows the complexity of politics in the Middle East. Or was it just an excuse to get in? This move was eventually supported by the Arab States after many negotiations in-between. My parents and many others truly believed that having the Syrians come in to restore peace meant that the war was over. It was during this time that they decided to go back to Lebanon.

PINE FORESTS, VILLAS, AND BOMB SHRAPNEL

When we arrived in Lebanon in 1977, we initially lived in a beautiful rented villa in an up-and-coming area called Rabieh. Located in the foothills of Mount Lebanon about a half hour from Beirut, Rabieh was dotted with gorgeous villas situated in the midst of pine forests that overlooked the Mediterranean Sea. Nestled in these lush hills was our new home.

It felt huge to me. I was seven when we moved in, which may have had something to do with why it felt so big. The entrance alone was large enough for us to roller skate in. And each morning, it felt like I had to go for a long walk just to get to my parents' bedroom. When we first moved in, there was little furniture. This house with three lounge rooms felt overwhelming. I don't ever remember it feeling like a home.

The villa was perched at the top of the world's steepest driveway that required a prayer each time we would drive up or down it. And the only close neighbours we had lived at the very bottom. We'd say hello, but we weren't on visiting terms per se. It wasn't like I could just pop in when I felt like I needed some company. Which truthfully, was often. They didn't have kids our age either. Rabieh felt lonely to me. Aside from playing with my siblings, I don't remember much else of this house, nor do I remember how long we lasted there. It couldn't have been more than a year…if that!

When the war got a bit testy, it was necessary to leave Rabieh for shelter and safety. We stayed with relatives in Jdeidet al Ghazir, where my two great aunts lived.

Returning home to Rabieh, we would find bomb shrapnel scattered on the rooftop of the house and throughout the forest. Parts of the forest were burnt down, blackened and scarred. The neighbours told us horrifying stories, like how their son could have died had he been in his bed when a piece of shrapnel landed right on it.

I honestly found these stories a bit too dramatic. Seriously! The son wasn't dead, so why go on about it? Well, as it turned out, they experienced the terror of being bombed, where we hadn't. The reason they went on and on about it is because they needed to process what had happened, and part of this processing was to talk about what could have been the worst-case scenario. My seven-year-old self just wanted to play, not process.

To this day, the war does not in and of itself elicit any explicit, traumatic memories for me. I remember running around with my brother and sister, enthusiastically picking up pieces of shrapnel and saving them as if they were some piece of beautiful memorabilia. It was what surrounded the war that had a bigger impact on me. Not to mention the subconscious stuff that happened along the way. Bombings were commonplace. It was simply how life was growing up in Lebanon in those days.

During the bombings, Mum was very cool-headed. Not

dramatic in the slightest. Give Mum a crisis and she shines. Calm, cool, and collected with a clear head. It was post-crisis we all worried about. By then her nerves were in tatters.

Then there was also my fear of thunder. It terrified me more than the war. When thunder struck in Lebanon, it sounded like an atomic bomb was exploding. The first time I heard it, when we were in our home in Rabieh, I was paralysed with fear. How anyone could ever get used to that, I had no idea. Give me bombings over a Lebanese thunderstorm any day!

After some time, the household conversation turned to finding a permanent home. The war raged on. And my father wanted to return to his roots. He wanted to live close to his mother in his childhood village on the Mediterranean Sea, Bouar.

SUNSETS, FISHERMEN, AND VILLAGE LIFE

Bouar was located just under thirty kilometres north of war-ravaged Beirut. When we arrived at the end of the 1970s, it was still a fisherman's village that had just seen its first four-story building erected. There were quite a few apartments for sale, and Mum and Dad were eyeing one on the third story. It was right across the road from the beach, with a gorgeous view that directly overlooked the Mediterranean Sea. My parents ended up buying that apartment.

I loved the view of the sea, its rock formations, blow holes, and the gentle sound of the tide rolling in and out over the pebbles. In the mornings, we would wake to the fishermen's boats coming back home from their night's catch. Before long, watching the sunset was taken for granted, as was watching the sunrise from behind the mountains on the east side of the house. This house was one that truly felt like a home to me.

Moving from upscale Rabieh to Bouar wasn't such the romantic move back then, however. It didn't feel cool to go to school in upscale Rabieh and then travel home to the village. If I had only known what an upscale move it really was! Perhaps then I wouldn't have felt so ashamed about living there.

Mum might not have brought back much furniture from Australia, but she did bring something else: five sets of Encyclopedia Britannica. She even had a special book cupboard built for them. The furniture in this house was super chic. Very modern art deco. As always, Mum kept an impeccable house and had plants everywhere. She'd often rearrange the furniture just for a change. On these occasions, it would always feel like I was entering a new home, and always gorgeously done.

Mum had incredible fashion sense. She was barely thirty when we moved to Bouar, and was truly stunning. Stylish. Regal. Men would fall at her feet wherever we went. Sometimes, she would take me shopping with her and let me decide which outfit she should buy. This was something that not only built my confidence early in life, but was also where my absolute love of fashion was born. She trusted my opinion and admired my taste from a young age. It was a foundational part of our relationship, one that has undoubtedly, in some way, shaped the woman I am today.

When she was out shopping, I would wait for her to come home and show me what she'd bought. As soon as I heard her toot the horn, signalling she was home, I would run to the balcony to see how many bags she had with her. She would then spread out all her new clothes and shoes on the bed and show me how they could mix and match. I idolised her in this way, and remember these occasions vividly.

When my parents had a special occasion to attend, Mum would get her hair done for it. She would choose Dad's clothes for him. He never seemed to mind; in fact, I think he liked it. He had to look good for her. For society. Going out in Lebanon was a classy event. Seeing them off was always exciting.

As much as a part of me felt like Bouar was home, there was also a big part of me that felt like I didn't fit in. The villagers all referred to us as 'The Australians,' setting us apart from Dad, who was born and raised here. Dad, however, was in his element in the village. Everyone knew him! It seemed that every other person we'd come across was his first, second, or third cousin. He waved and smiled at everyone who passed him. There was a guy in the village, Tony, who struggled with cerebral palsy, making it difficult for him to walk or talk normally. We'd pass him by in the car, and Dad would just give him the rude finger, as if he was strong enough to be one of the boys. He loved it. I remember him beaming with joy because of Dad's complete acceptance of him.

And don't forget *al atrash woo'l akhras,* which directly translated into the 'deaf and dumb guy' (literally what he was called in those days) who we always saw walking his cow up and down the village road. Dad greeted him with the same enthusiasm he did everyone else, and the man responded in kind. I adored this side of my father. But there was a downside to his love of everyone. One year, soon after we arrived in Bouar, he went on a three month trip to Australia. I missed him terribly, counting the days till he returned. But as soon as he walked through the door, he had a village welcoming committee, as is customary in Lebanon. He barely noticed me, giving his attention immediately to the visitors. I felt so rejected, and I promised myself never to miss him that much again.

Many years later, I was in Lebanon on holiday. Not yet

even twenty years old, I remember seeing Tony, who was now getting older and weaker. He had fallen over in the street across from our house, and the neighbours who came to help me lift him back onto his feet didn't hide their thoughts about the way his family 'neglected' him. According to them, he should clearly not have been allowed out of the house in his condition. I was shocked that this poor man had to listen to their cruelty. All I could do was show as much kindness as I knew my dad would have shown. Dad would have cracked a million jokes and then taken him home personally, even if it meant being late for dinner. This is why everyone loved Dad and why he was so adored. Dad could have easily won the 'villager of the year' award, but when it came to being a father and husband, he was absent and unavailable, busy attending to other people's needs. He sought the approval of others over the approval of his wife and family, leaving us feeling resentful.

Back in the '70s, the village was still a village. So very untouched. There were orange orchards, small banana plantations, and bamboo that thrived in the salty, humid air. I remember finding myself drawn to the villagers who had chickens in their backyard, a pot on the stove boiling away, and lots of people coming in and out. Our house might have been beautiful and fashionable, but it was, at times, lonely. Mum may have yearned for intimacy, but in her home she loved (and needed) her space.

On the occasions that we did have people over, it was always a sophisticated affair. Mum would get it catered, have someone help her in the kitchen, and she would dress up beautifully. I remember Dad would beam with pride when Mum entertained.

He had one hell of a woman, and she made him look damn good.

However, oftentimes, his children did not. I was still a bit of a tomboy and preferred hanging out with my brother and his friends. For entertainment, we'd throw the church bell rope up so high that it would get stuck on the rooftop. They had to bring in a special ladder just to get it down! I also remember us ringing the bell when it wasn't Mass hour, just to confuse the villagers.

Talk about shame being brought upon my father! We were known as 'Maroun's children.' This was said with a slur of contempt, which we wore as a badge of honour. They were just peasant villagers after all, and we were 'The Australians!'

These were the days of childhood rebellion. The crème de la crème of this particular time in our life was when my brother decided to make a tiny bomb under my teta's house. He took some sort of bottle and stuffed it with gunpowder, which I'm sure he got at the milk bar. He fashioned a fuse from a box of tissues. When lit, this tiny bomb sounded like a massive bomb, which of course scared the living daylights out of all the villagers. Not the sound you want to hear in a war-torn country like Lebanon.

My brother was shocked when Dad, bypassing his usual parenting style of giving him a beating for acting out, calmly sat down with him to discuss the seriousness of the times we were living in. He was told how lucky we were to have friends in high places. If not, Dad could have been put in jail for what my brother had done. Lebanon was under militia rule at that time, which meant that parents could be put in jail for the misdemeanours of their children.

My older sister was truly the embodiment of rebellion. Perhaps this was the curse of the middle child, but I personally think it was just an inherent personality trait my sister possessed. She feared nothing, and her actions did not go unnoticed by the villagers. Dad would get so embarrassed when someone would judgmentally say to him, "Oh, I saw your daughter roller-skating down the street smoking a cigarette." Dad may have wanted to focus on the villagers, but my brother and sister made sure they got his attention, any which way they could. Infuriated and publicly humiliated, Dad would come home and lose it at my sister for her rebellious ways. Not that this ever stopped her. I believe it actually made her more defiant. As for me, I was Miss Goody Two-Shoes. I would do anything to avoid getting in trouble. Dad never scared me, but one look from Mum could put the fear of God in me. Mum was a force to be reckoned with, and while I didn't fear either of my grandmothers, so were they. Teta Olga, especially.

Once upon a time, our little hillside village was a closed circuit. There was one road in and one road out. My Teta Olga's house was positioned strategically at the bottom of the road. Once all her housework was done (to the point where you could literally eat off the floor), she would sit outside on the balcony and greet each person that came in and out of the village. My teta was built-in village surveillance. If you were a stranger, questions were sure to be asked. *Who are you? Who are you here to visit? Why? When? How?* I'm sure she was a bit subtler than that, but then again maybe she wasn't. With Teta Olga, what you saw was what you got.

I was on holiday in Lebanon from Australia years later and remember being followed home to my grandmother's house by two young men. Somehow, they knew there was an 'Australian' in town. While being the token Australian gave me what I used to term 'superstar' status in Lebanon back then, I still felt creeped out by it. Not unsafe, but definitely harassed. I pulled up my car and quickly ran inside to tell my grandmother about it, and she immediately came to my defence. She stormed out onto the balcony, shaming them and shooing them away. I felt so protected and safe. That was how she showed her love.

She had some great sayings that still live on with me today. I recall asking her if such and such a thing was shameful. Her answer was simply, "*Aaib aalla elleh be oul aaib,*" or "Shame on those who say shame." On another day however, you could find her shaming away with the best of them. Such it is with the old Lebanese grandmas.

Then came the day of sad progress. There was a freeway being built from the north end of Lebanon to the south. The beach road that had given people access to both ends of the country was now simply too small to deal with all the traffic. This freeway cut straight through the village and was built right next to my grandmother's house. I don't know how my grandmother handled this, nor how she slept through the noise that got perpetually worse as the years slipped by. She was literally sleeping on the side of a freeway.

People from Beirut and its surrounding areas were starting to become interested in this quieter, safer side of Lebanon. Apartments and land in the village were bought up quickly. There was also another road built that allowed entrance to the village off the freeway. No more surveillance from the Village Queen. Plus, the village was now becoming more of a town, and the authenticity was slowly eroding, as was the calm of our once sleepy, little village. But it was here in Bouar that some of my fondest childhood memories were made. The colour of my life, be it dark or light, emerged during these years.

DRY CLEANING, DOG FIGHTS, AND MEZZA

Tip Top, Dad's new national dry cleaning business, was huge. It was more like a factory than any kind of dry cleaning business you might see today. It used to service all the hotels in Beirut and was the only dry cleaning business of its kind in Lebanon.

Dad, however, was busy being the ever-so-wonderful village man in business. You can take the man out of the village, but you can't take the village out of the man. Clichés die hard. Dad's staff adored him, and loved having a smoke with him. How Dad could make something as ordinary as a dry-cleaning business a busy social hub, I'll never know. But important people, from celebrities to politicians, who needed their expensive clothes dry cleaned, all popped in. And they loved talking with Dad.

Back in those days, I loved going there. The machines were enormous! My favourite one in particular could iron a king-sized sheet flat out. My sister and I would join in on the production line where two women stood at either end of the machine. On one end, two women fed the sheet through, and on the other end, two women had to catch the sheet and fold it perfectly to a point. It was then handed to one last woman who would do the final, three-way fold, put it on the stack, wrap it in plastic, and label it.

To this day, my older sister and I can look at each other and signal that we need to fold a sheet or blanket. We assume position on either side of the sheet and fold it in sync without a word. If I were to fold a sheet with anyone else, they'd surely accuse me of being a perfectionist! They simply don't understand the sheet folding pride that was instilled in me at such an early age.

A fabulous part of the business was the stretch limo the company owned. One night, we took the limo to a home belonging to one of Dad's business partners. This particular visit was memorable for reasons other than the stretch limo. We were sitting out on the balcony, having some mezza, and watching the dog fights (two planes trying to shoot each other down) in the sky, like it was entertainment. I vividly remember Beirut was roaring that night, as there was some serious bombing going on. And there we sat, watching as if it were fireworks on a live action movie. This all just seemed like a normal night in Lebanon, though. One that was filled with conversation and debate about the war. It was simply our reality.

EDUCATION, SUFFERING, AND HUMILIATION

There are two kinds of education systems in Lebanon: the French system and the English system. We went to The Evangelical School in Rabieh, part of the English system, in which we studied many of the main subjects in both English and Arabic. French was our third language. Being so young, I was able to pick up on the different languages quite quickly.

In Lebanon, you are shamed and humiliated for not doing well in school. It was hard for me to see my brother and sister get in trouble for not doing well. The risk of any kind of humiliation must have put the fear of God in me, because if I had a test, I would get up at four in the morning to start memorising every last word in the book. For a time, this granted me perfect scores on most tests and exams. It also sent me to the top of my class. While this made me look good, it really pissed off my brother and sister. But while they slept, I memorised. I was terrified of the consequences of not doing well. If not humiliation, then a possible beating. My siblings had no idea of my suffering!

At one point, the teachers thought I was doing so well that they suggested I move up a class. My older sister threw a fit. She refused to be in the same class as me, so thankfully, it never happened. I was more crushed by my sister's rejection than not moving up a grade. I would have loved to have been in the same class as her. I looked up to her rebellious ways. I thought she was cool. And yet, she wanted nothing to do with me.

All this made my parents so proud, you would have thought they were doing the work themselves. I would never wish the Lebanese educational system on my worst enemy. I think the parents often suffer more than the children. I understand that the Lebanese get an excellent education, but I simply can't justify the humiliation and suffering that goes with it. Later on in life, though, I met handsome Lebanese men who could speak fluent English, Arabic, and French...and found it quite sexy. Suddenly, the Lebanese education system didn't seem so bad.

As strict as the Lebanese school system could be, it was no match for my brother and sister. They kept getting into trouble at school. Eventually, my brother went to boarding school. This broke his nine-year-old heart. My parents thought they were doing the best thing for him. Perhaps the school system was also taking its toll on them. Either way, I really missed him!

At the Evangelical school, the principal had a yearly practice of going around to each classroom to praise the children who did well and to humiliate the students who did not. My sister had struggled with her marks this one year. So when he came to her classroom and asked her to put out her hand so he could hit her, in front of the whole class, she refused. For that defiance she paid the price of having to move to another school, which was even more oppressive. This new school thought they could beat education into children, literally. This would only further fuel my sister's rage.

And then there was me, left to go to my uptight school alone and oftentimes bearing the brunt of my siblings' resentment.

BIRTHDAY PARTIES, BOMBS, AND BELONGING

Although I felt at home living in the village, it created isolation from my friends, who mostly all lived in the vicinity of Beirut. I remember once when I was invited to a birthday party near Beirut, I was told it was too dangerous to go because of the shelling. I was devastated! I wanted so much to belong to the group. Bombs or not, more than anything, I wanted to go to this party. I convinced myself that my parents were just being too lazy to drive me. In reality, the war was raging, but this wasn't what I saw. Instead, I felt like an outsider with the girls at school. There simply weren't enough social occasions that would allow me to feel like one of them.

When it came time for my own birthday party, I was convinced no one would come. I was so ashamed that we lived in a village! Forget about the gorgeous view of the beach and the stunning sunsets. It was still a village. But to my shock, they all came. Parents and all. I begged Mum to make hot dogs and party pies, but she had to go all high society on me, which meant catering to the parents. She made a full buffet more suited for a Sunday lunch than a ten-year-old's birthday. I was so incredibly embarrassed. All I wanted was a kid's party, like the ones I was familiar with in Australia.

SHELTERS, MASSACRES, AND NIGHTMARES

It was rare that we needed to take shelter during the war in our part of town. The village was safe. Refugees from Beirut would flee to our village for shelter. Around 1980, however, there were rumblings going on between one Christian militia headquartered in Bouar and another Christian militia headquartered in Safra, Bouar's neighbouring village. Word got around that things could get a bit dangerous during the night and that it would be best to take shelter.

Our neighbours had better shelter than our exposed four-storey building, so we went down to their house to be safe. At ten years old, it felt fun to all be huddled together. I wanted that feeling to last forever. At some point, however, Mum decided that she would prefer to die in her own home rather than be cooped up in a box for safety. So back home we went. I felt sad that we had to leave and that there was so little commotion. As if it were all for nothing!

We woke up the next morning and got back to life as usual. We saw only a small amount of damage to a couple of houses on our way to school. It felt very anticlimactic, to be honest. Not much was said about it after that, but I was mortified to learn many years later that some eighty-seven men died that night, the 7th of July, 1980. In an effort to consolidate all Christian militia fighters, a massacre had taken place at the various militia bases, including the Safra militia headquarters just a few kilometres down the road, and it barely got a mention.

Though consciously I often felt the war was anticlimactic, on a deeper level it did affect me. I had a recurring nightmare, if you could call it that, as it happened during the day. I would mentally plot and plan on where I would hide if an enemy militia came through our building slaughtering us or gunning us down with their *Kalashnikovs* or *M16s*. These machine guns were household names.

I kept hearing about the various massacres and slaughterings that took place here and there. Some stories became etched in my brain. In particular, the ones of pregnant women having their stomachs slashed open to make sure their babies died as well, and of Palestinians being tied behind a car and dragged down the street. These stories filled me with terror and trauma. Their justification for killing the baby? There would be one less Palestinian in the world. The hatred ran deep.

So I decided on a good hiding place for when the time came. It was common for most homes in Lebanon to have an attic, *tetkhiteh*. That would be my hiding place, I had decided. I would quickly jump onto the washing machine and climb up into the *tetkhiteh* and hide. Sadly, it would have been one of the first places the militia would look, but I was barely ten years old, and my plan was unsophisticated.

Years later, I was staying with a family in Dubai as an Airbnb guest. My host was also Lebanese and had grown up in Lebanon during the time of war. As it turned out, we had the same recurring nightmare. Stories can terrify us just as much as reality can. I sometimes think that they can sink deeper into our psyche than we realise. It's only later that they rear their ugly heads.

MISSILES, MARINES, AND MEMORABILIA

In June, 1982, when I was eleven years old, Israel launched a full-scale invasion of Lebanon after an assassination attempt on the Israeli ambassador in London. The initial aim was for the Israeli Defence Force (IDF) to push the armed Palestinian Liberation Organisation (PLO) out of South Lebanon, creating a 25-mile protection radius. This would ensure missiles could not be launched into Israel from south Lebanon, therefore protecting northern Israeli communities. The IDF, however, pushed on further than their initial 25-mile radius, reaching the outskirts of Beirut. Eventually, the PLO surrendered and were given protection in Tunisia.

During this time, when I would wake up and go out to the balcony and look out towards Beirut, I could see black patches still smouldering from the bombings the night before. Soon after, an air force base was set up by the Lebanese Forces on our side of town. The war seemed to be moving across the country, closer to us in Bouar than ever before. This air force base eventually became a target for the Syrians, who every now and again would send missiles flying our way. You could hear the missiles coming by the whistling sound they made. Then the whole sky would begin to rumble, indicating that they were getting closer.

My brother would hear the missiles first and lead us out to the balcony with jubilation. How desperately we wanted to see where the missiles landed! On one occasion, we got to see a few plunge into the Mediterranean Sea in front of the house. Such an exciting time in our young lives!

Mum, on the other hand, would be freaking out. Looking back, I can't blame her. Leaflets were sent out that instructed us to hide in the stairwell if we were under missile attack. This would ensure there were more walls to protect us. While we were heading out to the balcony to look for missiles, she was losing her mind trying to get us into the stairwell.

The excitement, however, started and finished within minutes. And it was always followed by a bit of disappointment that not much happened. We were privileged in the sense that the war didn't immediately touch us in any physical way.

This was also around the time Israeli army tanks peacefully rolled down the beach road in front of our house. The Christian Phalanges had partnered with the Israelis to push out the Palestinian and Syrian militia, so we had new allies, the Israel Defence Forces. There we were, out on the balcony saying, "Shalom," to soldiers as their tanks passed through. It felt weird greeting the Israelis in this way. Many of their attacks on Lebanon were disproportionate in nature, killing thousands of innocent civilians on our shores. But here was their military right in our own front yard with a promise to protect us, when not long ago the Syrians promised to provide the same kind of protection. It was not always easy for me to keep up. They soon moved out however, handing over most of the land they'd invaded to the South Lebanon Army, a Christian Militia.

As Israeli forces began to move out, the peacekeeping forces began to move in. The Multinational Force in Lebanon (MNF) was deployed to assist the Lebanese Armed Forces in the 'peaceful' withdrawal of the PLO, the Syrian forces, and others involved in the war up to that point. It wasn't uncommon to see U.S. Marines, British Guards, and French and Italian forces out and about wherever we went.

Despite Lebanon being a country riddled by war, the coastline was becoming littered with new resorts. One of these new resorts was Saframarine. It was in the neighbouring village of Safra, where less than a couple of years before, the massacre had occurred. It was a mere ten-minute walk from our home. Brand new and nestled right on the beach, it was both intimate and beautiful. It had a bowling alley and a wax skating rink. Finally, somewhere fun to go on Sundays.

We had secret crushes on the peacekeeping forces that shared our new space at Saframarine, but my sister was more into them than I was. I was still shy, and she was a bit older than me. Plus, shy was not a word that fit into my sister's vocabulary whatsoever. I remember she had a denim jacket with heaps of different badges on it. She would ask the Marines to give them to her. And what were they going to say to this gorgeous Lebanese teenage girl except yes?

Life in the village was beginning to wake up from its slumber. Who knew how many peacekeeping forces were called in? Thousands, I know now. Back then, however, I just remember liking the presence of so many different types of people in town. Truly a collision of East meets West. How different things had become!

PRESIDENTS, ASSASSINATIONS, AND RETALIATION

The country was buoyant this summer of 1982. For the first time ever, we had a presidential candidate that the whole country was falling in love with. He was young, handsome, and so charmingly charismatic. The nation hung on his every word. At six o'clock each night, we would gather around the television to watch the news, and not a sound was allowed. The adults didn't want to miss a word.

His name was Bachir Gemayel. He was the commander in chief of the twenty-four thousand men that made up the Lebanese Forces. His presence on television was strong. Commanding, yet understanding. It was easy to see why he had earned the respect of the people.

In one of his speeches he argued that the time had come to have a president that wasn't only asked for by the Lebanese people, but was accepted by them as well. His speeches spoke directly to the heart of his people: "Even if Syria, even if Egypt, even if the Vatican, and even if America wants a particular president…but the Lebanese people didn't find that president suitable, he should not be allowed to be their president." He had a way of talking to the people, and the people welcomed what he had to say with open arms. Lebanon was at war, and Bachir knew that the Lebanese president had to be Lebanese first. Not a Maronite, not a Sunni, not a Shia, not a Druze.

He strongly stood for all armed foreign presence (Syrian, Palestinian, American) leaving Lebanon and was steadfast in his desire to see the liberation of our country. He became wildly popular worldwide, and when he was elected in August, 1982, Lebanon was jubilant. New hope was born. Finally, a president that stood for Lebanon first and foremost!

This newfound hope, however, was short lived. Devastatingly, less than a month later, a bomb exploded in the Beirut Phalange Headquarters, killing Bachir along with twenty-six others. I woke the next morning to see the curtains drawn back. Mum broke the news to us. The house was dark, and the air hung silent and thick. As if there hadn't been enough darkness already. This day of mourning was etched forever into my eleven-year-old mind. Within days, there was a retaliation for Bachir's assassination. The Sabra and Shatila Massacre was an event that would result in thousands of Palestinians and Lebanese Shiites being brutally massacred. Revenge was the only language left.

RESORTS, BEACH PARTIES, AND PUNKS

My siblings and I lived in the Mediterranean Sea for four months out of the year. I knew every last stone and rock at the bottom of the sea. When Mum wanted us to come back home, she would put a towel out on the balcony. At night when it was hot, I would go to sleep on the *balancoire* (swinging couch) and rock myself to sleep to the sound of the waves washing over the pebbles. For some, it may have sounded like noise, for me, it was like a lullaby.

In summer, it was suffocatingly hot and humid, so many opted to go to the mountains in search of dry, cool air. Others had a chalet or a cabin at a beachside resort. For the children, the resorts provided real summertime fun. On Sundays, they would be jam packed with families eating and swimming.

Given Lebanon's terrain, it took between thirty minutes to an hour to get to cooler weather, which was found one thousand metres above sea level. We could go skiing and come back to the coast in the same day, where everyone was still on the beach.

By 1983, the instability in the country had reached a new level of intensity. Two suicide attacks seemed to be the cause of the shift in the political tide. One suicide attack was on the U.S. embassy, killing 63 people in April, and the other was in October on the headquarters of the peacekeepers, killing 241 U.S. and 58 French troops. But in Lebanon, war never got in the way of a good time.

With death knocking at the door every day, living in the moment was all the people had. During this time, there was a huge influx of families fleeing Beirut into our safer side of Lebanon. This influx brought a new vibe to our village that was like nothing we'd experienced in our first few years growing up there. Bouar, as well as our neighbouring villages, not only offered a safe-haven, it offered a fabulous summer life. Saframarine was now in full swing, women strutting their stuff in their bathing suits and high-heeled shoes. Stunningly gorgeous with perfect bodies and perfect tans, fluently speaking three languages.

This is the year that changed my experience of living in Lebanon.

Boys began to notice me, and I had no idea why. In my mind, I was the boring little sister! The last thing I thought about myself was that I was attractive, especially compared to the glitz and glamour of the girls from Beirut. I had thick eyebrows, a gap in my front teeth, and short hair. Not to mention I was painfully shy. At almost thirteen, I was just thinking about being friends with boys. Maybe that and an innocent kiss.

A popular boy from England, with the most gorgeous blond hair, started giving me attention. Apparently, he wanted to give me so much attention that he decided it would be cool to show me his hard-on while we were roller skating. I was mortified.

No one had prepared me for something like that. But I still liked him. Maybe because all the other girls had a crush on him, and it made me feel special to get his attention, as gross as the whole thing was.

The Saframarine Resort wasn't the only thing happening in our once sleepy village. Small chalets became increasingly prominent up and down the coast. A new source of income for the villagers. Some of them were mere shacks, while others had a more glamorous touch. Before long, they were everywhere. Our little village was quickly becoming a hip part of town. We were surrounded by the style, fashion, and funk of Beirut. Yachts floated lazily along our shores. There were beach parties, new foreigners arriving, and plenty of boys.

It was an awesome time to be an almost teenager in Bouar. Along with the invasion of the Beirut style came the punk culture. I remember Mum taking my sister to the hairdresser, and she arrived home with the coolest punk hairdo ever. I was devastated. She was so cool, and by comparison I felt like such a nerd.

In the midst of the war, the government had decided it needed to build a bridge to ease up the traffic on the way to Beirut, and my dad's dry-cleaning business was in the way of plans for the bridge. War was certainly not getting in the way of progress. The government was going to pay my father to be able to demolish his dry-cleaning business. Many a court-case had to be attended to resolve the legalities. But somehow, each time the court-case was set, there would be some religious holiday, and given the number of religions in Lebanon, there were many delays. Each delay put further pressure on my parents. With the war raging in Beirut causing the schools to shut down, and business life being disrupted, our future was uncertain in more than one way. War raged even further in our home. Just to tip my parents over the edge emotionally, the Lebanese pound depreciated 3,000 percent, rendering any payment my father got inconsequential. The pain of losing so much of what my parents had worked so hard for was shattering for them, and the fights were shattering for us kids. With the war intensifying inside and outside of our home, and with life in Lebanon having little foundation, the decision to return to Australia was made.

The news was devastating for me. I had finally fell in love with living in Lebanon. That summer however, would be my last. And I was heartbroken. From then on, the yearning to return rarely left me.

ATTENTION: GIVE IT TO ME

If there was one thing about leaving Lebanon I was happy about, it was the fact that I would not have to suffer the educational system any more. School had been getting harder, and I knew memorising everything was not going to work for much longer. I found myself praying the war would get worse so they would close the schools. That way, I could avoid sitting my exams. The war did get worse, and the schools did close, leaving me feeling like the worst person on the earth, as if I had wished death on people just so I would not have to sit exams.

To top it off, I rarely got attention from my parents when it came to school anymore. It was as if my perfect marks bored them. They stopped putting my tests up on the fridge to show me how proud they were, and instead my siblings always got more attention because of their struggles at school. During the last year of school, I gave up worrying about humiliation; it was attention I wanted and needed. So my new strategy was to not try as hard anymore.

Just before we left for Australia, we managed to find a safe time to go to school to pick up my report card (despite not sitting exams). I got straight Ds. I was certain that would get me some attention. Mum glanced at my report card and simply said, "I know you can do better than that." I was outraged and desperate for real attention. Her reaction worked, though. From then on I went back to doing well at school.

MODESTY IS A WASTE OF TIME

By late 1983, we arrived back in Australia. There was quite a bit of acclimating to do, to say the least. First, there was the full-cream milk and cream buns you could order at school. And let's not forget to mention the beloved Aussie pie soaked in tomato sauce. These were my simple pleasures, and overnight I went from the skinny child who never finished her food to a bit of a fatty who stuffed her face with milk, cream buns, and meat pies. Thankfully, vanity kept me from continuing in this way. Adjusting to a new culture that had long been forgotten came in strange ways.

I recall going to a new friend's house after school one day. Her mother made a comment to her friend about my 'big black eyes' as they were having coffee. I felt humiliated! I thought they were talking down to me and that having black eyes was something to be ashamed of. I thought they were referring to me as ugly. I had no idea that something as common as my big, black Lebanese eyes could be seen as beautiful.

I was a bit sensitive, however. We were the only kids at our high school who were ethnic, after all. When we walked through the playground at school, they would chant, "Lebon, Lebon, Leb-a-non." This was the year Australia was promoting the benefits of drinking milk, and there was that damn ad on

TV that had the jingle, "Live on, live on, live on milk."

For a while we sucked it up. My older sister, however, wasn't so patient when it came to being so blatantly mistreated. If I remember correctly, she pushed a girl who was giving her a hard time, and she fell back onto a window, shattering it. I silently loved the way my sister didn't take shit from anyone! Mum was no stranger to the principal's office. She was the one that had taught us not to take shit, but then had to deal with the repercussions of our actions. Not something always easy to do. Mum also felt the sting of racism in Australia. And it hurt.

This racist existence lasted until my sister and I went to Sacred Heart College in 1984. We were no longer the only ethnic kids, but we still discovered the girls in Australia were different from Lebanese girls. In Lebanon, girls bragged about how beautiful they were. To hear a woman say something like, "I don't know what he sees in her, I'm so much prettier," isn't uncommon in Lebanon. The girls in Australia, however, complained about how ugly they were! I once made the grave mistake of saying something nice about myself to one of my 'friends.' She responded by saying, "Gee, you're modest, aren't you?"

I became known as the Lebanese girl that was 'full of herself.' Instead of fighting what these girls said about me, I embraced it. No matter how hard I tried, I just couldn't buy into the whole self-deprecating thing. To counter this attack on myself, I coined a couple phrases. "If you've got it, flaunt it," was one. And the other? "Modesty is a waste of time." I taught these phrases to my friends and encouraged them to love their ethnic beauty. When blessed with Mediterranean genes, why not embrace it?

However, all the while I was encouraging my friends to embrace their beauty, I didn't actually relate to myself as beautiful. Honestly, I was too busy noticing how beautiful my friends were. I truthfully considered myself to be ugly. Any natural beauty I'd inherited was oblivious to me. It wasn't until later in life that I learnt how to embrace my beauty, power, and intelligence without deflection. Something else I learnt? Embracing your beauty, power, and intelligence is a matter of choice, not a matter of fact.

TORN BETWEEN TWO LOVERS

When we lived in Lebanon, I dreamt of living in Australia. When we returned to Australia, I dreamt of living in Lebanon. I missed the action. The people. Sadly, I even missed the news. I could never understand why people went on strike in Australia. What on earth for? There were no bombs being dropped. Couldn't they just be grateful for living in their perfect, safe, benevolent country?

I missed looking out at the sea. I missed watching the cars go by on the beach road. There was always something going on in Lebanon. Yes, there was a downside, but the upside of having a community around was something I had definitely taken for granted. And as annoying as the community had sometimes been, at least it was something. I even missed having neighbours that pissed you off one day, but the next day, you were back in each other's pockets. There was human interaction. There was life.

Australia felt so empty…benign. To me it was boring and slow. There was no energy. Nothing ever happened. In Australia, there was only ever one beat: Perfect. At least this is what it felt like in Geelong. In Lebanon, summer guaranteed fun. In Australia, you had to wait for the weather to be nice to even realise it was summer. And then you still had to drive an hour just to get to a good beach.

As for my education in Australia, I never really felt like I got one. It all felt like pretend. In Australia, school curriculum was so easy, it felt tedious. They called me the cool nerd because I was intelligent, yet apparently still 'cool.' But I started to feel like I didn't belong with my friends as I was never in the same classes as them, so I stupidly dropped out of advanced math class to do what we called 'Vege Math'—math for vegetables, the running joke amongst my friends. It was yet another cultural difference I faced with the pull between the two countries I was raised in. In Australia, intelligence is seen as nerdy. In Lebanon, it is revered.

HOLD THE ONIONS, PLEASE

When we settled in Geelong, Dad bought a café, and I loved it. It was called George's Café and was the only café open on the weekends. I was passionate about flipping hamburgers, making a mean souvlaki, and frothing the milk to make cappuccinos. Joy was found, slicing tomatoes, onions, and lettuce. Pride was found in buckets overflowing with prep for the evening rush.

My sister and I ran the café on the weekends. We were fourteen and fifteen. A friend of ours came to work with us, and the three of us had so much fun. Those days hold some of my fondest memories of growing up and being in Geelong. Café life wasn't easy for a teenager, however. We missed out on other fun, like going to the beach with our friends and lazing about doing nothing at all. We never complained, though. To us, it was normal.

I loved the pace of café work, especially the peak hour rush. I could take an order without writing a word of it down. It didn't matter what it was. No onion, extra cheese, hold the sauce, extra mayo. I got it. My mind was made for retaining this information. Go ahead and be as fussy as you like—my dad taught us to do it the village way by getting to know our customers personally. He had always been more about the people than doing good business.

My sister and I would arrive some mornings to find piles of dishes that didn't get washed the busy night before. This was always a sure sign that Dad had stayed late tending to the drunks that spilled in after the nightclubs closed. But we didn't complain. That was just Dad. But this trait drove my mother crazy. There's a certain wiring that gets set up when you work on demand like you do in the café world. In hospitality, you have to be on.

Years later, when I upgraded to being a waitress, I would pride myself on being able to get a nasty, grumpy customer to smile. The worse their mood, the more of a welcomed challenge. I still love café life to this day.

When your parents own a business, the conversation is always about the money. The takings, the expenses, the profit, the loss, the this, the that, the blah, blah, blah. I can remember cash on the dining table being counted, sorted, and spent. Our life was simple and working just fine. Until, of course, my dad's eldest brother started to get his nose in things and made it his life's mission to get Dad to sell his profitable little café and buy a pub in Melbourne. He would even back him financially!

My uncle believed that owning a café was now beneath my father. All Dad's brothers were buying up big in Melbourne… and making serious money. But it was café life that was most suited to Dad. So when he finally caved in to his brother's pressure and bought a pub in Melbourne, life eventually started to fall apart.

BABY SISTER...THE ANSWER TO MY PRAYERS

Around this time, Mum fell pregnant. I was fourteen, my sister fifteen, and my brother sixteen. We were all so excited! Mum was extremely inclusive about the whole thing and even allowed us to decide on our baby sister's name. But one day, way too early…her water broke.

She was only six months along. I vividly remember standing next to her as she called the doctor. Dad was in Lebanon on a business trip, and I recall seeing the fear in my mother's eyes. And even though I wasn't aware of the extent of the danger, I knew something was seriously wrong. Mum was rushed to the hospital from Geelong to Melbourne. There was a feeling of excitement, finally a bit of action. But then the reality of the situation began to sink in.

Given that my sister was three months early, each day Mum could hold off giving birth was another day my sister had the opportunity to grow bigger and increase her chances of coming into the world. This was 1985, remember. Medicine has come a long way since then. Somehow, though, every day gave new hope of survival.

The decision to have a natural birth or a C-section came

too quickly. Not even a week had passed. Both ways presented a risk. As amazing as the body is, there was still a chance that both Mum and the baby could die in the process. And as much as Mum believed that the final squeeze of childbirth allowed the baby to feel safe, a natural childbirth was going to be too dangerous. The infection Mum now had could spread during a natural child-birthing process, and if this were the case, neither would make it. So things went from mildly dramatic to very serious in a matter of days. For the baby's safety, the decision was made that she must be born Caesarean.

And then she arrived. My beautiful baby sister, who weighed in at only one kilogram on the day she was born. I will never forget the first time I saw her. I had waited so long, and now here she was with a tube down her throat so she could eat, and wires attached to her little body to make sure she stayed alive. When she cried no sound came out. She was so, so very tiny. So tiny in fact, that no one expected her to make it, but she did. My little sister was a miracle.

So how did three teenagers handle this very delicate situation with Mum and baby sister hanging on for dear life while Dad was in another country? We did what any healthy teenagers would do. We threw a party. My brother was turning seventeen, so we thought to celebrate. We literally had bands playing inside and out. Everyone came. Even the police a few times! And while we didn't sit and speculate about it as such, I'm sure this party was about us acting out. Life was short. Our sister and Mum had almost died!

In those first, very critical days when my tiny sister would not put on weight, the nurses assured Mum that one day she would be like all the other girls, worrying about losing weight! Mum was amazing, especially taking into consideration that Dad didn't make it back in time for the birth. Mum and my little sister were back in hospital in Geelong by the time Dad finally returned from Lebanon. We have a picture of his ring on my little sister's arm with half the space still left in the ring. It was truly hard to comprehend how small she really was; more like a doll than an actual human being.

Mum had to stay in the hospital until my baby sister was healthy enough to go home, which of course made her crazy. She got to the point where she would refuse to let the nurses use the tube to feed my sister. She couldn't stand the savagery of that damn feeding tube.

Finally, Mum and my little sister arrived home. Mum was almost always hooked up to her breast pump so there would be enough milk to feed my sister. She ate so little! If Mum didn't do this, her milk would have quickly dried up. It was breast milk that made my sister's chances of growing healthily all the greater. Poor Mum. As a teenager, I couldn't figure out why she was always so stressed and angry. I was just excited to have this baby sister. As a kid, you just don't get the full extent of the seriousness of the situation. So Mum's outbursts would, as always, cut like a knife.

BOYS, BRAKE LIGHTS, AND EAR BASHINGS

The party we threw after our little sister's birth had me star struck with all the gorgeous college boys around. But my brother had done the whole overprotective Lebanese brother thing and told them if they touched me he would kill them. I found this out much later, however, so at the time, I was left wondering why they would barely speak to me. As if I had the confidence to date one of them anyway! They were way too cool for me. Still, I felt like killing my brother for that. He was supposed to be my ticket to boys, but instead he cut off the supply!

My older sister was everything I wasn't. As always, she was going wild. She wanted to go to a party that my parents wouldn't let her go to, so she stole my grandmother's car and drove there herself. But unbeknownst to my sister, the brake lights were out, and she got pulled over by the police. Mum found all this out because she sensed something was wrong and listened in from the upstairs phone when my sister was telling one of her friends about it. And when Mum complained to my sister about how ashamed she was going to feel about having to show up to the police station with her, what was my sister's response?

"Don't worry, Mum," she said. "All that will happen is that I'll get an *ear bashing* from them."

Mum's response was priceless. "What, you'll get hit on the ears?"

You've got to love it! My sister and all her cool, and my mother for being oblivious to the Aussie slang.

But we were teenagers. And we were acting out. It was normal. I was jealous that my older sister always got the attention, though. She was so much fun, breaking the law and whatnot. God, why was I so boring? Miss Goody Two-Shoes all the way. Homework and good grades were my focus. You'd never find me stealing my grandmother's car to go to a party.

Good girl or bad girl, Mum was still absent during this time. She was exhausted from her brush with death and her constant worry about my premature sister. There was little energy left for my brother, sister, and me. Over these years, tension rarely eased between my parents, but with yet another move to come, things would escalate to a whole new level.

THE WRONG MOVE

Eventually, Dad bought a pub in Melbourne. The Star Hotel. A live band hotel. I was sixteen, and despite our Lebanese culture, my older sister and I were not sheltered from pub life. We naturally switched gears from making hamburgers to perfecting pouring a beer. In this regard, our parents built our resilience. And when push came to shove during the early hours of the morning, my inner strength and confidence showed up in strange ways. I had no fear breaking up a fight between two drunks. I would put myself between them and get a bit Dad-like using humour to diffuse.

My very favourite part of The Star Hotel was the piano bar. At the end of a shift, we would all sit around the piano and sing. The space Dad created at that hotel was one of intimacy and togetherness. Camaraderie. As usual, the people that worked for Dad related to him as a friend rather than a boss. Today, this kind of behaviour would be a sign of good leadership; it was good management, however, that was lacking.

By now, most of my uncles had transitioned into the pub and nightclub scene in Melbourne. The economy was booming, and they rode the wave. It was the '80s, and my uncles were on fire. It honestly felt like they owned the whole town. What a feeling!

Along with all the glitter and glam of making it big came something else: family politics. The divide that was created between my uncles during this time was heartbreaking. At a time when they could have banded together and created an empire, some turned on each other instead. Each wanted to prove that they were right, or smarter, or victimised. Some parents forbade their children to be traitors, and did not allow contact with other cousins. My parents would say, "The children should not get involved," but there was always an undertone, or a guilt, associated with going to the 'enemy's' house. This, of course, broke my heart, and my cousins' hearts, too.

While my uncles were soaring in business and making obscene amounts of money and buying gorgeous homes, clothes, and going overseas…we were going broke. The pub industry, let alone the music industry, required experience that Dad simply didn't have.

My dad knew cafés intimately, considering he'd been working in them since he was sixteen years old. The overheads were more contained, whereas the expenses for a band venue like The Star Hotel were huge—thousands in rent per week, repayments to the bank, wages, hiring bands. There was simply more complexity and higher expenses. Dad was out of his depths, and each week the business fell further behind. Financial ruin was knocking at our door.

ROCK BOTTOM

It was a harrowing year of financial stress our family had yet to experience. Each day, the conversation revolved around potentially losing everything, including our home. That thought would terrify me. Unfortunately, Dad had mortgaged every last asset he and Mum had owned, which was madness, given such a risky investment. This was news to Mum! I was used to war raging in our home, but to have the threat of homelessness and full financial ruin was yet another level. It was my final year of high school. The tension at home was too much for me to handle. My parents had moved to Melbourne, and I was now travelling by train to Geelong. I had to leave the house at 5:30 a.m. to get to school on time. I lost interest in my studies as I could no longer see what the point of anything was. I went from being the top of my class to barely making it through my final year. Yet again, my mother reminded me that I could do better. I seethed at the lack of acknowledgement of how impacted I was by our toxic home environment.

At my mum's bursts of outrage, Dad would defend himself, saying he felt like he had a noose around his neck. He knew he had messed up, and every fight he had with my mother further tightened the noose. She was beyond angry. Life felt out of control.

Eventually, the business was sold, losses were added up, and somehow by the grace of God, we got to keep our home in Australia, as well as our childhood home in Lebanon. But all else was lost. Paying the bills and buying food became a weekly strain on the household.

I remember sitting down with Mum to sort through the whole mess. A nightmare to say the least. The stress and anger that arose in Mum were becoming too much for me to bear. So I repressed these feelings by helping even more. As clear as my mind was about the best ways to work through our unfortunate situation, I was completely unaware of the emotional impact it was having on me.

Worrying about my parents' financial well-being weighed down on me. I believed it was my job to help them sort through it all. They were in pain, and try as I did, I could not separate myself from it.

I feel for that young part of me. What about her? Her dreams? Her life? Where was she going? I was harsh on myself for doing so poorly in my final, and very critical, year of high school. I felt like such a failure. What was I supposed to do now that I'd messed up my exams and couldn't get into university? Nothing inspired me. I felt so lost and needed someone to help me find my direction. Help from Mum or Dad was clearly out of the question at this point.

My brother would say to me, "I saw you sitting in the car today. You looked so depressed! What do you have to be depressed about, Cindy? You're smart and beautiful and intelligent. You have the world at your feet." At least he saw my pain. But I needed empathy. A word that was simply not in our vocabulary.

RED EAGLE, KYLIE, AND CIVIL WARS

Given the circumstances, my older brother and sister and I went to work to support the family. At a minimum, we would not be a financial burden to our parents. With all the stress, Mum needed to get away. She went back to Lebanon with my little sister, who was now four years old. I can't say that I blamed her. And it honestly came as a welcomed relief. The house just felt so much better without the tension between my parents.

During that time, one uncle in particular came to the rescue. Uncle Lee. He was in his prime, flying high with wealth and happy to share his good fortune with others. He gave Dad his dignity back, offering him a job and a way out of the hell hole he had dug himself into. This uncle renewed Dad's confidence in himself. He went out and bought new clothes. He looked stylish, instead of crushed. Dignified, instead of degraded.

Dad flourished working for someone else. He managed other people's business with greater clarity. He knew his stuff, and he had learnt painful lessons. Now, without the burden of the entire responsibility, he became a good operator.

My uncle also gave each of us a job. My brother and I worked at one of his inner city Melbourne nightclubs, the Underground.

I then worked at the Red Eagle Hotel in upmarket Albert Park, and eventually, he trusted my siblings and me with running one of his pubs, The College Lawn Hotel in trendy Prahran. This uncle has always held a special place in my heart because of his generosity. These were some of the hardest years in our family's life, and he was there when others weren't.

Although home life was more peaceful without the constant fighting, I quietly resented Mum for leaving. I understood why she needed to go. It was a matter of sanity. But what about me? While in many ways it was better that she had left, I was still young and really needed Mum to help guide me through this time of my life. But how was Mum to guide me when she couldn't even guide herself?

While she was away in Lebanon, civil war broke out between the Christians. It was one of the worst conflicts, and while we were accustomed to civil war, we weren't accustomed to fighting between Christians. The war had now crossed over into our side of town. War was right on our village doorstep. Brother against sister, brother against brother, and friend against friend. Households were divided. For the first time, we had casualties in our village. Horror stories of people we knew being splattered to death against walls.

Mum had picked a terrible time to take a break, and I feared I would never see her or my little sister again. It was the first time ever that news of the war in Lebanon scared me. Somehow the distance evoked greater fear. When we finally did get to speak to Mum, however, she spoke about it as if it were some sort of adventure! Talking about her plans for escape from Lebanon via Syria, dismissing our fear as if it was nothing. Perhaps she was trying to alleviate our fears, but all I remember was feeling extremely angry with her putting herself, and especially my little sister, in danger.

Work became a welcome distraction from my fears. Whilst working at the Red Eagle Hotel, Kylie Minogue had her twenty-first birthday party there. I was working the bar that night. Seeing her walk through the front door with her entourage felt surreal. She was tiny, which did not match her large celebrity status. I was expecting something amazing to happen that night. I was so excited. But the whole thing felt a little anticlimactic. Up close, these celebrities had much less of a magic air than I would have expected. This night made me realise that being a celebrity didn't mean much at all. They were just people, no different than me.

After working at the Red Eagle Hotel, I joined my brother and sister at the College Lawn Hotel. Without a doubt, these were some of the most fun times of my young life. I developed a love of playing billiards. There was a dedicated billiards room where I had a blast playing with and against the boys. The clientele at the College Lawn were around my age, and most went to the ultra-prestigious Wesley College that was just around the corner. I quickly found out that, just like being a celebrity, being wealthy didn't seem to take away problems either.

Apparently there were some problems that seemed to touch every family, including my own. The only difference was that in other families the parents got divorced. Amongst my extended family, divorce was unheard of. Back then at least, divorce was simply not an option no matter how bad things got. The social stigma and judgement surrounding it was too high. Some of my customers at the College Lawn however, came from families where it was perfectly normal to get a divorce, and they would share how it made them feel. They hated their step-fathers and hated going to counselling. I was so jealous! While I didn't want anything to do with the stepparent part, I desperately wished I could go to counselling. These were very painful years for me. Having someone to talk to about the way I was feeling would have been warmly welcomed.

I wanted my feelings to count. To have someone realise how empty I felt. How directionless I really was. How different my life might have turned out if I had someone to talk to during that time. If being a celebrity didn't make much of a difference, and neither did having a lot of money, what did? Mostly, I just craved being seen. To have someone embrace me and tell me, "Everything is going to be alright. This is normal. You will get through it. Tell me how you feel, sweetheart. I'm always here for you, no matter what."

With no adult to guide me, I turned to men as a place of refuge. Now, the fantasy of 'love will heal all' became my drug of choice. Even if love was not manifesting in the moment, at least I could fantasise that one day it would, and then everything would be well in my world.

Feeling directionless, I would talk to some of my customers at the pub about my confusion around what to do with my life. The energy of the hospitality industry can be amazing, with regular customers becoming like close family. I had one regular at the College Lawn who really took the time to listen. And it was he who gave me the simple advice to go back to school and finish my studies. He could clearly see there was more to me than being a bartender.

I wasn't thinking about what I would love to do for the rest of my life. I was thinking about stability. Financial stability. I ultimately decided that accounting was something I was good at. And I was at a point where I desperately needed to feel good. I needed to feel safe. Secure. Accounting offered all of this. Off I went to complete my Associate Diploma in accounting, which would be my ticket into university. Finally, something to put an end to the shame around barely scraping through high school!

ESCAPE

Whilst Mum was away, I had managed to get permission from Dad to go on my first overseas trip. I was nineteen years old and off to America. An event that coincided with Mum's early return home from Lebanon. None of my friends nor my cousins were allowed to travel, and I saw no point in waiting for someone to join me. So I decided I would travel alone. I needed my own escape. A change in scenery. So as soon as I had the money, I booked my flight to Hawaii and then Los Angeles. I was over the moon with excitement. But then Mum came home, and all the peace and quiet we'd been enjoying for the past few months quickly disappeared.

She was furious that Dad was letting me travel alone. What kind of father was he? It was okay for her to go to war-torn Lebanon with my four-year-old sister, but I couldn't go on a trip to sunny Hawaii? There I was though, with Dad's permission to fly halfway around the world for my first solo adventure. It was here that my anger towards Mum started to spill out. The good girl act was diminishing, and I retaliated in full force to her protests against my trip overseas. In my biting teenage tone, I told her she couldn't just come back and play mother when it was convenient for her. Deep down, I was pleading for her, silently screaming at her, to tell me why she hadn't been there when I needed her most. Regardless, when I make up my mind to do something, I can rarely be stopped. So off I went.

As difficult as I found travelling alone to be, I toughed it out. And as the years went by, I learnt how to do it better and better. Travelling was to become yet another escape. A release from the mundane. The monotony. An escape from the aimless misery.

DEFINED

I am a young woman
I am not broken
I will show you

Shame hates it when we reach out and tell our story. It hates having words wrapped around it—it can't survive being shared. Shame loves secrecy. When we bury our story our shame metastisizes.

— Brené Brown

As long as you keep secrets and suppress information, you are fundamentally at war with yourself...

— Bessel van der Kolk

SEWING MACHINES, FLAMING LAMBORGHINIS, AND A BIT OF CHEMISTRY

Despite returning to my studies, I couldn't find any inner peace. I was still lost. Bored with my education. On the outside, it looked like I was doing so well. Getting almost perfect grades and working on top of it. I had enough money in the bank. The joke was that Cindy would make six hundred dollars and save seven hundred. I was terrified of poverty and saved everything I could. But I was deadly bored. Being good at something does not mean it makes you happy.

Accounting was crushing my soul. But what else was I supposed to do? Fashion designing? Dancing? Yes, I wanted to be a Solid Gold dancer. Who didn't? It was my love of fashion, however, that expressed itself more readily.

From the age of fourteen, I would sit at my sewing machine for hours and make my own clothes. I could get lost in a fabric store, sifting through all the patterns, looking for beautiful fabric. I couldn't draw to save my life, though, and applying to the fashion schools required a portfolio. Forget it. Not to mention I was constantly reminded of how hard it was to get a job and make money as a fashion designer. I reasoned that one day I would simply have the money to buy all the clothes my heart desired, and it would alleviate that yearning to create and make my own clothes.

Work was my only escape from the boredom and agitation I was feeling. I was working only one night a week at the Paladin nightclub. It was truly an amazing space. Back then it was a marble masterpiece. Marble, marble, and more marble. There were waitresses to cater to the customers' every need, as well as someone to shine your shoes. Very much the high-class establishment.

I came alive when working at the Paladin. My agitation eased during my shift, and I had all the company I needed. My bartending mate and I had the perfect chemistry. That right mix of tension and friendship. We performed quite well together behind that bar, lighting it up with flaming cocktails and entertaining the customers with our fiery relationship.

Things at home were tense once again. Back to the constant arguing over money, and the back and forth bickering between Mum and Dad. I was getting seriously depressed and didn't know how much more I could take. I recall sharing my feelings with Mum. I told her I felt suicidal. She told me that she felt the same way! I felt desperate, with nowhere to turn. So again, I just shut my feelings down. It was too painful to deal with all alone. It also did something else. It entrenched in me the deep feeling that I was the only one I could count on. That I was all alone. That there was no one to turn to but myself.

PEACE, PARTIES, AND WAR-TORN SIGHTSEEING

To escape my misery, I planned a two-month trip to Lebanon. As it turned out, I wasn't the only one who wanted to return back home. The war was over, again, and Lebanon had peace for the first time in almost fifteen years. It was a country exhausted from war. Parents allowed their children to live like there was no tomorrow. It was a seventies-like sexual revolution, except it was in Lebanon in the '90s. Everyone trying too hard to be cool, modern, and hip.

Lebanon was suddenly somewhere to be again. Many that were studying in London, Paris, Rome, and other faraway places in the world began to return. And with them they brought the distinct style of whatever city they came from. Stylish Italians, classy Brits, sophisticated French, and hip Americans. It was a wonderfully eclectic time. Everything was alive, and everyone wanted to embrace being Lebanese once more. I couldn't have been happier with my heritage.

A childhood friend, a neighbour who lived just across the road from us growing up, was kind enough to take me on a tour of all the destruction that had taken place during the last Christian civil war. When in Lebanon, I suppose! There was a town nearby that experienced some of the worst destruction, so that is where she began. I was shocked. Gutted. Sickened. It was once a town full of gorgeous villas and a place of distinguished society…now it was flattened to the ground.

There was something different about seeing this destruction. Seeing Beirut smoking and all but destroyed was one thing, but I was shocked by the devastation in this once beautiful upmarket place that was on our side of town. It was as if my inner-world was also flattened. So much for running from the war raging in my home. This was the real deal. This was what happened when anger truly ran its course. Nobody won.

When I returned to my grandmother's home that day, I felt sick. I wasn't able to get out of bed. I simply couldn't process my feelings. I felt empty, and once again there was no one to turn to. What was I to say to those who lived through it? "Oh, I am so shaken by the devastation I saw today?"

It was a case of denying my own grief, because, of course, it could not possibly be as bad as theirs. I didn't live through it. They did. It would be years before I would attend to my grief with the honesty and attention it deserved. In the meantime, I did what every self-respecting Lebanese war survivor did. I repressed these hollow feelings and did the best summer partying I possibly could.

I was at one of the new resorts with a family friend, and I was bored. There is only so much sunbaking I can do without going out of my mind. And there was one of the lifesavers, eyeing me up and down every chance he got. He was so forward, unlike the aloof Australian men who, at times, lacked a pulse. Why not go along with it? I was curious to see what happened. It wasn't long before we casually started to see each other. It filled in the blanks of my lonely existence. Despite life looking like it was fun with lots of comings and goings, emptiness was still my constant companion.

But this kind of 'fraternising with the resort staff' was not a welcome choice, it seemed. It did not go over too well with my friends. I couldn't figure out why. Apparently in Lebanon, lifesavers aren't of a high enough social standing! This confused the hell out of my Australian mind. I was on holidays. He was cute, kind, and attentive, and at the age of twenty, that seemed to be a good enough criteria. My friends, however, kept trying to set me up with the 'right' kind of guy. But I ignored them, thinking their idea of 'right' was all wrong for me. This was just a holiday thing. Little did I know that I couldn't have been more wrong.

WHEN ARE YOU GETTING MARRIED?

One of the first things Dad asked me when I returned to Australia was if I was going to marry this guy I'd been seeing back in Lebanon. Married!? I was barely twenty years old. Getting married was the last thing on my mind. Experimenting, yes. But married, no. What Dad didn't ask was if I was happy. If I was compatible with this boy, or if the relationship was nourishing me.

My agitation got worse after I returned home. Perhaps it was all the marriage talk. Regardless, I simply couldn't settle. Life in Australia wasn't resonating with me in the slightest. Lebanon may have traumatised me on one level, but on another level I felt alive. And it was my birthplace.

I had one semester left in my accounting diploma but could not even see it out. Instead, I planned to move back to Lebanon for a whole year. I already had a job lined up, I had money saved, and I had my parent's house in Lebanon where I could stay. It seemed like the perfect plan. So once again I packed my bags and headed back to the Middle East.

LIFE FELT SO GOOD

That time in Lebanon was one of the happiest I had ever known. It was a relief to have space from all the fighting at home. I had the house all to myself. I was working. I was studying French. I was in a relaxed relationship with my summer romance, Ajwad. It was easy and provided a nice balance of companionship and intimacy. I would sometimes come home to find a bag of freshly picked oranges hanging on my door. It wasn't a huge love affair, but it was kind and caring.

Life was simple and easy. I felt content. Until Mum and my sisters came to town. On one hand, it was nice to have family close by, but on the other hand, my life started to feel stressful again. With Mum came all her angst about Dad. There was simply no escape from family drama.

My older sister quickly found out where all the cool people liked to hang out. She befriended them. She was living on the edge, while I was dating a boy no one approved of. My little sister was in over her head at her new school trying to learn Arabic, German, and French. Mum needed support. Maybe Dad could come to tame his daughters? He couldn't. He was busy helping my brother set up a business. But, as if out of nowhere, respite came knocking at our door. A blast from the past. A childhood friend of Mum's from her heydays in Beirut.

He had just driven past my grandmother Olga's house in the village. How he knew it was her house is beyond me, but two-degrees of separation makes anyone easy to find in Lebanon.

He had stopped to inquire about my mother and asked my grandmother to send his regards to her in Australia. She told him that he could do that himself, given that my mother was actually in Lebanon. In the village, in fact. My grandmother pointed him straight to our home. I opened the door to find a version of Danny DeVito in front of me. He soon became a regular fixture in our home, providing Mum with a temporary distraction from her two eldest daughters. He was hilarious and fun to have around. When Mum, her best friend from school, and Danny DeVito got together, it was a joyful event. I had never seen my mother that happy. I felt both happy and sad at the same time. Happy to see my mother joyful, yet sad for all the years I'd seen her in tears. In Lebanon, surrounded by her Beirut friends, Mum was different. In Lebanon, I was different.

But for as much contentment as I had experienced when I first got to Lebanon, life there was losing its appeal. I did not feel like I was making much of my life. And the stress of being in a relationship no one approved of began to take its toll. Life, you could say, wasn't going so well anymore. So I quit my job. I decided to break up with my boyfriend. I was ready to return to Australia once again. But it was not anywhere near the way I would have expected.

I remember the night. A summer night in Lebanon, a few weeks before I was due to go back to Australia. Danny DeVito, Mum, Mum's best friend, my boyfriend, and I all went out to dinner to a beautiful restaurant in the mountains. Ajwad and I knew we were breaking up, and for a reason I will never be able to explain, that night, we weren't careful.

There was an unmistakable energy that came over me that night. The kind that cannot be put into words. As if the energy of your child comes to you even before he or she is conceived.

For the next few weeks, I patiently waited for my cycle to prove me wrong.

DAMAGED GOODS

Three weeks later, that powerful feeling came over me again. I was late. I just knew I was pregnant.

I pulled myself out of bed and walked apprehensively into Mum's bedroom. I climbed into bed with her, seeking comfort and safety.

"I need to talk to you," I said quietly, my voice rising barely beyond a whisper.

Finely tuned into a mother's intuition, she asked, "What, are you pregnant?"

I nodded, not believing what I was about to say. "Yes, I think so."

Here is the irony with Mum. In situations such as this, she is amazing. Rather than shaming me, she permeated the moment with a gentle calm. Rather than chastise, she went out and got me a pregnancy test. When the results instantaneously revealed what we both already knew, and I dropped to the floor, my Mum stayed composed and took me tenderly in her arms.

I was in shock, sobbing. "I'm so sorry, Mum. I'm so sorry."

She held me close. "Don't cry," she said softly. "You'll hurt the baby."

She took me into the lounge and sat me down, her eyes full of compassion and strength. She was so calm, while I sat terrified. I felt sick, helpless. And while I don't remember all the details of our conversation on that day, we did begin to discuss the options I had.

But let's face it. In my culture, there were only two options. Get married or have an abortion.

The thought of having an abortion left me feeling dead. It was as if in the moment I knew I was pregnant, I was instantly connected to my baby. This connection I felt, however, did not keep me from praying to God each day that I would miscarry.

Fear took over. I was unable to function with any clarity whatsoever. I felt paralysed, like I had completely ruined my life. There was no escape from the dread that gripped me.

And then there was Mum. Calm in the face of the storm. Clear as daylight. Practical. She started suggesting options.

"Do you think Ajwad would marry you?"

I shook my head. "I don't know," I answered, sobbing. Did I even want to marry Ajwad? I had just broken up with him. Now, I was carrying our child.

"You can get married and go to Australia," Mum suggested. "Ajwad can work in your brother's café."

I stared at her blindly. Feeling numb. Praying that this was all a bad dream.

First things first, we had to get a proper pregnancy test. But in Lebanon, people wait for the tiniest bit of anything to create gossip. A neighbour in our building worked at the hospital, the one and only place to get such a test. And there was Mum, seeking out a pregnancy test, concerned people would think she was pregnant when my father wasn't around. They would have a field day with that one!

I don't know how, but I do know that Mum took care of it...and was glowing with the results. "Yes," she said. "You're pregnant."

She was elated, and though I was grateful that this was her reaction, I was also confused. She went straight into fix mode—something I needed, and appreciated—but at no point did we discuss how I felt, why it had happened, or what I really wanted to do. So I remained numb trying to deal with the panic and devastation that overtook me.

But she was amazing in how she dealt with it, given her upbringing, our culture, and the possible wrath she would get from Dad and society.

Now all I had to do was go and tell my ex-boyfriend.

Ajwad's family had cherry and apple orchards high up in the mountains. He was there that day. I had been there many times, however, I'd never taken the drive by myself. I surprised myself by finding it easily, awed by the brilliance of the land that surrounded me. For a moment, I forgot why I had come. I drove past a waterfall, then down to his family's property, which sat on the edge of a cliff overlooking a stunning valley below.

It was there I found him, watering the orchards on a magnificently beautiful day. He wore his farming clothes, sweating in the midday sun. And when I looked in his eyes and told him about the baby, I remember how happy he was. How he took me tightly in his arms while we cried together. I will always love that side of Ajwad. His joy was unmistakable. He could not have been happier.

Ajwad drove down with me, back to Mum's house. The three

of us sat together, and by the end of a conversation that felt like it took years to have, we agreed that Ajwad and I would marry and move to Australia.

In what should have been an exuberant experience, I felt my life crashing down around me. All my dreams gone. In an instant. How could I have been so stupid? I felt no happiness, only dread and despair. I had ruined my life, and I was ashamed. Never had I felt like this before. Never had I felt like such damaged goods.

Mum was amazing through all of this. Not for a moment did she make me feel ashamed. For her, having a baby was nothing to be ashamed of. The Lebanese culture, however, can be unkind. And though Mum had a high tolerance for the dysfunction of her culture, she was ahead of her time in terms of having an open mind.

It was her open mind that made her want to shield me from the often unfriendly society of which we were a part. And to be fair, she also wanted to shield herself from the cutting tongues of those who surrounded us. I felt angry that we would have to care so much about what other people would say, but this was her community, and she would have to continue to live amongst them. The need to hide my 'situation', however, filled me with more shame. It was a shame so deep that all I wanted to do was find a way out.

Still, the 'situation' had to be faced.

I HAVE NOTHING TO OFFER YOU

Ajwad went home calm, yet returned the next day looking solemn. Terrified, was more like it. He had spoken to his brother in America…who told him he was crazy. And who had also put the fear of God into him. What was he thinking? He had no money. No education. Nothing to offer.

While one cannot blame an older brother for looking out for his younger brother's best interest, I couldn't help but think that Ajwad was weak for listening to his brother. My fear crippled me, and any deviation from our plan of getting married and moving to Australia caused me to shut down even further. I was angry and felt little compassion toward Ajwad. In my eyes, my life was ruined. And though I'd fully played a part in it, I had no room for anyone else's fear on top of my own. It was all just too much.

The situation began to crumble around me. Ajwad begged me to have an abortion. He pleaded for my understanding. At one point he even got romantic about it, saying we could have a baby together at a later time. Had he forgotten our recent break up?

I felt sick. Terror had completely taken over my world. My

head was constantly spinning, and I felt crushed, petrified, and panicked in what seemed to be every moment of every day. All I could think about was how much I had screwed up my life. Dreams shattered. Hope for the future all but gone. I didn't want to marry Ajwad, but I also didn't want to get an abortion. Once, in my all-girl Catholic school, I'd been sick the day the others had to watch a documentary on abortions. When I returned to school, they shared with me the part in the documentary that showed the aftermath of an abortion, the bits of the dead baby discarded in rubbish bins. I was never able to get this image out of my head from then on whenever I thought of abortions. But I needed to fix this mess, and with no marriage, abortion came back into the conversation.

With Ajwad's mind changed (and my true feelings of not wanting to marry him acknowledged), I still could not fathom the thought of returning to Australia and raising my child as a single mother. In fact, that option barely crossed my mind. I could not face Dad, single and pregnant. That was too much shame to bare. And I was not ready to have my situation be the latest family gossip. They would be cruel.

I have often questioned why I didn't take this option more seriously, but at the time, I lacked any clear conviction. I was too consumed with my shame and self flagellation, not to mention the fear of raising a child alone. *How could I have let this happen to me?*

Those early days of the pregnancy now blur together. Ajwad was freaked out (appropriately so), but I hadn't the strength left to continue to discuss things. Mum, still the rock, stepped in and was firm with him. Not unkind, but firm. She told him it was fine if he didn't want to marry me, but she would take over from here on. She led him out, and I truly believed I would never see him again. To be honest, it came as a welcome relief.

The next day, however, he returned. By then, I simply couldn't deal with him. I needed someone strong, but that was unfair to expect of him. We were twenty-one and twenty-two respectively, and while I wasn't fifteen, I was still terrified, and so was he. Still, I had no energy left to give him.

I told Mum I could not speak to him. And she, of course, was wonderful with him. Ajwad was completely overwhelmed. She took him aside, while I sat out on the balcony staring at the sea. I sat there dazed. Numb. Virtually catatonic.

Mum, with the amazing strength she used to carry us both through this time, told him we had decided to get an abortion. Ajwad was devastated. He sobbed and begged for it not to happen.

Mum was gentle with him. She comforted him, allowing him to release the heavy emotions he was holding on to. She calmed him down, and supported him the best way she could. He eventually left. I didn't see him go. I was so self-absorbed, indifferent to all but my own feelings, that I didn't have any room to worry about how he felt. I was the one who would bear the brunt of it in our society anyway. I would be considered loose, the irresponsible one. It was I who would be deemed reckless. Never the other way around.

Abortion was illegal in Lebanon. This simple fact did wonders to add to the sheer complexity of the situation I found myself in. And it deeply intensified the anxiety I was already living with. In this time, not a word came out of my mouth. I felt hollow, a shadow of the person I once was.

Mum saw how cold and shut down I had become. She knew I didn't want the abortion. She knew I didn't want to get married. And she knew *we* did not dare face the option of me becoming a single mum. I felt trapped. Frozen in the mid-summer heat.

Clearly, the only option I had was to get an abortion.

Being in the orbit of Lebanese culture, I didn't think the same way I would have if I had been in Australia. In Australia, I would have turned to my friends. I could have received counselling. I could have looked at *all* the options. I would have been given space to make a clearer choice. But that was not my reality. We weren't in Australia. We were in Lebanon. And here there were only two options to be spoken of. Now, all we had to do was figure out how to get an abortion in a country where abortion was illegal.

AND SUCH BEGAN THE REST OF MY LIFE

How quickly life changes. Where just a couple of weeks before I was breaking up with my boyfriend and trying to figure out what to do with my life, here I was looking for a doctor who would be willing to give me an abortion. In Lebanon, it's all about contacts. It was a case of Danny DeVito to the rescue. He knew of doctors that would be willing to perform an abortion. But these doctors had their own moral compass and said they would only do the procedure if I was not too far along. Mum and I left for Beirut the next day. Who had the nerve to wait anyway!

In the car, just as we were about to leave for Beirut, Mum said something about raising the baby ourselves, if it came down to it. This option was ever so delicately still on the table but still too far out of reach. Dad, who was oblivious to what was going on, would never have approved. I really think Mum would have liked to have been strong enough not to care about what he, or anyone else would say. She would have rejoiced in not caring about how others would criticise her parenting and blame her for her 'loose' daughter. Judged she was, nonetheless, over the years, the aunties and uncles coming down on her for allowing us certain freedoms.

We went straight to Danny DeVito's house in Beirut. A huge villa in the heart of the city. His daughter was there. It was our first meeting. She was visiting her dad from Europe and was gorgeous inside and out. I will never forget her support that day, comforting me as if we'd known each other our entire lives.

It was all so damn surreal! My mum and her friend were behaving like my parents, and his daughter felt like a long lost, loving sister. And there I was, sitting in an unfamiliar living room somewhere in the bowels of Beirut preparing to go through with an illegal abortion. When had life taken this sudden and huge detour? And looking back, why all the drama? I had created life. What was the sin in that? Culture! Damn culture!

As I sat there, all I could think about was that I was going to kill my baby. And while I have no judgments of anyone else having an abortion, I was suddenly living it and knew I couldn't do it.

Then, out of the blue, I was snapped back into the moment. Danny DeVito stormed into the living room like a ranting madman. He was screaming, he was shaking, he didn't want blood on his hands. He couldn't be involved with this clearly immoral act that suddenly had him seeking out which one of his doctor friends would take the life of my unborn child. I was shocked. What was this sudden change of events? As if I needed *more* freaking out! Didn't anyone realise *I* was already freaking out? It was Mum who then came gently toward me and asked if I really wanted an abortion. What was I to say? I shook my head. Of course I didn't.

Seriously, how much more could I take? All the complication. All the drama. When it came down to it though, the truth was that I just didn't want an abortion. It was not a logical decision, it was visceral. Talk about marriage re-commenced. But the question was, was Ajwad still willing to get married? Now the biggest problem was getting in touch with him. This was the early nineties, and there were no cell phones. So we did what we had to do and called my sister, who did not yet know I was pregnant. When she heard, she immediately burst into tears.

I think knowing my sister was upset made me somehow feel better. If only because it suggested that maybe she cared about me more than I thought she did. She was willing to drive to Ajwad's home in Byblos (*Jbeil*) and ask him if he would still marry me. How she found his house is one thing, but how he found us in Beirut is another altogether. There are no street signs or road directories in Lebanon. And although details as to how this all went down are hazy, before long Ajwad was in Beirut, asking me again to have an abortion. I was confused. Wasn't he there because I had decided *against* having an abortion?

We were out on the balcony, that familiar standard feature of most Lebanese houses and apartments. It was there that I asked him to marry me now and divorce me later. As much as I didn't want to get married, I couldn't stand the thought of my child being called a bastard.

In Lebanon, if you're not married when you have a child, the state doesn't recognise the child's existence. Any child born out of wedlock is not entitled to papers. No identity papers. No passport. And a life permanently being known as 'the bastard.'

Finally, he agreed to marry me. It felt like I'd had to plead. Beg a man I didn't want to marry, to marry me. It was humiliating. And such began the rest of my life.

OPERATION COVER-UP

Once it had been decided that we would be married and keep the baby, Ajwad stepped up. He was strong and convicted. As for me, my heart was cold. The disappointment and shame I felt were overpowering.

We began making plans to elope. DeVito's daughter was in charge of the flowers, while my sister and I looked for a wedding dress. We needed to find a hairdresser. I had to get my christening papers. It was lucky that I was born and christened in Lebanon. The last thing I needed was to get christened at a time like this. There is no civil marriage in Lebanon. The church reigns supreme. We had to find a priest that would marry us. We had to find a church. There was so much to do for something I was devastated to *have* to do. Ajwad led that charge. He knew how the system worked and seemed to sort it out with efficient speed. He emerged as a solid man.

In Lebanon, it's customary to go to confession before the marriage ceremony. So there I was, in the most gorgeous ancient cathedral in Byblos, *Jbeil,* where I was supposed to confess to a priest who was literally hitting on me five minutes earlier.

"So do you have anything to confess?" asked the creepy priest who had just finished eying me up and down.

Oh yes, I wanted to say. *I'm pregnant and want to get married to cover it up.*

Instead, I crossed my fingers and lied. Because, you know, if you cross your fingers it isn't a real lie! How much I would've loved to confess the truth just to get this damn secret off my conscience!

As it turns out, it was a blessing so many people believed Ajwad and I were such a mismatch. It made the cover-up so much easier. All we had to do was pretend that my family didn't accept Ajwad, and due to our undying love for each other, there was no other choice but to elope.

There came a point during all this planning and fussing that I felt sick to the stomach with it. I told Ajwad I couldn't do it. It was too much. I went to find Mum. She was having a lovely time at one of the nearby resorts. This triggered a deep yearning for my old life, where I didn't have to hide a pregnancy and marry a man I had broken up with a few weeks prior. When I told Mum that I couldn't go through with it she told me, in her very practical way, that everything would be okay. And then she sent me back on my way. What could I do but push through? I felt like I had no other option.

I asked Ajwad not to tell anyone about our eloping, but he needed some kind of support himself, I guess, so he told his whole family—but without telling me. When I arrived at the church, I was greeted by his entire extended family. I did not need an audience while I endured my shameful marriage. I was so miserable I found it hard to fake happiness.

My little sister was about seven and was the flower girl. But she felt something was wrong and started to cry. Others genuinely looked happy and were quite supportive. One of Ajwad's friend even gave us his BMW to use during our honeymoon.

After the wedding, a few of us 'surprisingly' showed up at Mum's house to 'break the news' that Ajwad and I had eloped. It was all so strange, Mum playing along, feigning shock…but just enough to not make it look overly dramatic. It was one of her finer performances indeed. After she got over her shock, she did the traditional thing of accepting our choice. We almost had a nice time. The day had its moments of comfort, safe at home with Mum. I savoured what was quickly to become no longer familiar. As if I instinctively knew just how dramatically my life was about to change.

Our wedding day slipped into the evening and we headed off to a hotel after we left Mum's. We had a marriage certificate now, so we were allowed to legally stay in a hotel—the law did not permit a man and a woman to rent a hotel room unless they were married. So off we went. Ajwad and I headed towards our 'happily ever after.'

I was devastated, but Ajwad seemed so happy. Genuinely happy. He was acknowledging of my strength in choosing to keep our baby. I was still shut down. Nothing Ajwad could have said would have made me see this situation in a positive light. There was no joy in anything. In my eyes, my life was over.

HUSBAND AND WIFE

For the month following our elopement, Ajwad and I stayed in a lovely little chalet in the mountains. It was beautiful. Surprisingly, I began to kind of enjoy myself. I felt settled and happy. And Ajwad was so good to me! When I got morning sickness that literally lasted all day, every day, and we couldn't mention it to anyone because we were still hiding my pregnancy, Ajwad would go out to get me whatever I needed.

He really was an involved partner, and I was honestly surprised someone would do all these nice things for me. I'd never had anyone do anything like this before, nor had I ever seen my father take care of my mother in this way.

Mum would come to visit often. She was so sweet and supportive. I loved having her there. It was comforting and felt solid, where for so long everything had felt shaky. I watched Ajwad transform before my eyes. He went from unfocused with little ambition, to becoming focused on becoming a good husband. He started working with his uncle in his plumbing business. And as Ajwad transformed, so did my relationship with his mother, albeit slowly. I went from the 'unsuitable Australian girlfriend' to being treated like her favourite daughter. It was confusing, to say the least. All of a sudden, this woman was my mother-in-law. It was such a huge swing I couldn't even begin to digest it all.

After our first month as husband and wife was over, we moved in with Ajwad's parents. They had a spare two-bedroom apartment downstairs from their own home. It was adorable. Perfect really, the way it overlooked a small orange orchard. There were chickens outside, and the landscape was gorgeous. I loved it. It all felt so peaceful and serene. I remember I wanted to decorate our little place and that I felt happy. But it wasn't how I had imagined my life would be.

My fantasy life, the way I had envisioned it, involved far more glamour than this. But as it was turning out, this life seemed to agree with me. It really was such a perfect place. I would get up in the morning when I pleased and meander down to visit Ajwad's cousins to have our own *soubheyeh,* mimicking my grandmother's morning ritual, but at a more respectable hour, usually eightish! After a cup of tea and some breakfast, I would then leisurely make my way back to our apartment and sit at my sewing machine. I made pregnancy clothes. It was honestly such a happy and simple existence.

Except, of course, for the hum of what people were saying about me. By now my pregnancy was public knowledge, and the things that people were saying began to get me down again. I pretended that I didn't care. I kept my head held high. But I cared. Sometimes, I wonder how things would have been different if I had been able to relax more at this time of my life. If I hadn't experienced the shame coming from those around me.

Oh, what a waste, they would say behind my back.
Such a shame.

She's ruined her life.

They had higher hopes for me. Still, their words felt cutting and cruel. But it was also what inspired my determination. I devised a plan. I was going to finish my education and get my life together. I would show these people that despite their shaming words, nothing would get in the way of my 'success.' This was the birth of my 'Fuck you, I'll show you' coping mechanism.

I NEED SPACE IN THE CUPBOARDS

With the news of my eloping, Dad soon arrived in Lebanon. Let's just say that all hell broke loose between him and Mum. I felt I needed to tell Dad the truth about my falling pregnant. I went to him one morning while he was still in bed, kneeling gently next to him. He told me he already knew. There was no shaming or anger. Only love. And that was the end of it.

After things calmed down between Mum and Dad, he picked me up like he never had before. I think he saw the terror in my eyes. He told Mum he was worried about me. And he took me aside, telling me gently not to worry about anything. He was not only supporting me in a way he never had, he was completely in tune when it came to my fear. As if he knew it so well.

With Dad's arrival, it seemed that Mum could relax and deal with her own feelings about my falling pregnant. Eventually, the reality of my situation began to settle in. And as calm as Mum was in a crisis, the aftermath was ugly. It was as if Mum's 'calm before the storm' had well and truly passed. She ordered me to collect my things from her house and take them to my own. Otherwise, she told me she would throw my clothes off the bloody balcony.

"I need space in the cupboards," she told me. It was as if she now needed to erase me from her life.

I was too much of a mirror for her. I'd done the same thing she had done. Made the same mistakes. Married the shepherd when I should have married the prince. As is often true in many families, history was repeating itself right in front of my mother's eyes. Her disappointment ran deep. I was crushed. Alone. Terrified. I vowed I would get myself out of this and never depend on my mother again. Or anyone else for that matter. Independent superwoman was born in one pivotal conversation I had with myself.

I will show them, I told myself. *I will never need anyone again. The price is just too high.*

SURPRISE!

Ajwad's Australian visa was taking longer to come through than expected. I had to get out of this shame pool I constantly felt I was in. I couldn't shake it. So at four months pregnant, I organised my flight to Australia and left without even a discussion with Ajwad. Mum and Dad stayed on a bit longer.

I arrived in Australia, lived with my brother and worked at the café he had now opened. Life felt quite nice. The worst of the morning sickness now gone, I was feeling the best I had since falling pregnant. Now it was time to get focused. I had a child to raise. I signed up for distance education. It was time to complete my Associate Diploma in accounting and get myself into university to get my degree. I had four subjects left. I would take on two subjects a semester and finish what I had started. No more being distracted by 'being lost.' I now had a clear focus. I wanted to be the best mother I could be.

My brother was great with me. He shocked me one day by saying, "I wish you had told me you were pregnant. I would have told you to just come home and have the baby instead of getting married." What had happened to the brother who was going to kill any boy that even looked at me? Since when was he so open minded? My brother bestowed such kindness on me. When I worked in his café and would feel dizzy or tired during the mid-lunchtime rush, he never got annoyed. He would insist I just sit down. Being great in a crisis was a family trait. I actually started to feel happy. I enjoyed this new focused life. I almost forgot I was married. Silently, I wished I wasn't.

Then one day, a month or so later, Dad arrived back home. Mum and my sisters stayed on in Lebanon. My little sister was at school, and Mum did not want to disrupt her school year midway. Dad thought he would surprise me by not telling me that Ajwad had finally gotten his visa and had travelled home with him. So with no warning whatsoever, Ajwad walked through the door behind Dad. It was too much reality for me with so little warning. I felt crushed. My happy little existence was now over. It was time to face the fact, again, that I was married. Ajwad noticed the look on my face. He, too, was crushed. He was all alone in Australia, and this was not the welcome he had hoped for.

FLOATING ON AIR

Mum, still in Lebanon, wasn't home for the birth. Her sister, my godmother, stood in for her. But without my mother nearby, I felt terrified and alone. To top it off, I had a horrible nurse. I told her I was in pain and she said, "This is nothing, it will get much worse." Seriously! I went into complete panic. My whole body must have tensed up. The labour wasn't progressing, so they had to give me drugs to help. Still, the birth took about two days.

And then came Alexander.

This love! I had never felt anything like it. It was thrilling, but such a shock! I always thought having children ruined your life. Hadn't Mum always damned the day she had children? But this. This was different. I couldn't take my eyes off him. The feelings were so new and so fierce that I went into panic that something would happen to him. What would life be worth then?

I also remember the guilt that washed over me as I held this precious child in my arms. *Dear God, please forgive me for ever wanting to miscarry or have an abortion*, I prayed over and over again. How could I have ever had such thoughts? This boy was a love I had never known. The strongest I'd ever experienced, and so unlike anything I could have ever imagined.

Mum and my sisters returned home a few months after. Everyone was enamoured with Alexander. I was floating on air after he was born. I felt the purest love. I wanted to give him everything. He became my reason for being. It was as if everything leading up to the day he was born now made perfect sense. I no longer needed to worry about myself. All my love and energy would be poured into being the best parent I could be. Alexander became my purpose. It was through my son I found life, love, direction, and focus.

LET'S STOP LIVING A LIE

Despite not being in the marriage of my dreams, for the most part I found married life to be easy. Ajwad and I worked well as a team, and our life eventually found a comfortable rhythm. And for a Lebanese man, Ajwad was very hands-on. He helped out around the home, not exactly the most common trait of a Lebanese husband. As it would seem, this life looked perfect to many people. At times even to me. So much so that I had almost forgotten I wanted out. The happy little family thing felt nice. I remember feeling so proud to have created a beautiful home. By the age of twenty-five, I had a good job and was almost through my accounting degree. My accomplishments were starting to nicely mask my shame.

But any time I tried to talk seriously with my husband about creating our future, he diverted the conversation to wanting to go to Lebanon or America. He had plans he wanted to pursue with his family.

Here began our biggest split. I had dreams, and I wanted to make plans with my husband. He, however, wanted to make plans with *his* family rather than *our* family. With no aligned future to move towards, a subtle separation began to take place.

And then, in one of those defining life moments, I found myself down in Geelong having a girl's night out with my school friends. Ajwad was at home with Alexander, and I was enjoying the freedom I'd quietly been missing. It was this night I met up with a childhood friend that I hadn't seen in at least seven years. The moment we saw each other, there was a chemistry that I'm pretty sure everyone around us felt as well. Old feelings returned.

He'd also had an unplanned child. He was exploring whether or not to get married and was confused about what would be the right thing to do. We sat close together, comfortable, as if we had known each other intimately for years.

"Do you love her? What about when your daughter is grown?" I asked. "How would you feel about being with her mother once your daughter turns eighteen and leaves home?"

And while we spoke, I began to realise that my questions for him were really questions for me. Questions I'd avoided. Questions I didn't have the time or space to explore. I felt like I was living a lie. The utter pretense of my marriage came crashing down on me that night. And I had to figure out what to do about it.

When I returned home, I started by asking Ajwad a question that would eventually change everything.

"If I didn't get pregnant, is this the life you would want to live?"

"No," Ajwad replied, without skipping a beat.

At least we were on the same page. I suggested we stop living a lie and find the courage to leave our marriage. We talked for what seemed like hours, and in the end, agreed that we both didn't want to be married to each other. It was that simple. But this didn't mean it would be easy.

Ajwad freaked out the next day. He didn't want to go through with it. Said we could make it work. I stayed resolute. The truth had finally come out, and I wasn't backing down. I was free. Free of the pretense, the lie. Something that had been missing for some time. The ability to actually act on our decision however, would take time. Apparently, while I wanted truth to dictate our lives, Ajwad wanted social appearances to rule them. This made for a terrible combination.

It was soon after this conversation that Ajwad's father died. Our conversation took little precedence in the face of death, and so we pushed it aside for some time. We moved house again instead. A real house, with a real backyard. The joy snuck back in...but not for long.

SHOOTING ARROWS

Life went on for a while as if we'd never had that conversation. We settled nicely into our new home. I truly loved that house. Alexander did, too. He had a cubby house in a tree in the backyard. We had dinner parties. It all felt quite sophisticated and sweet. Ajwad had recently taken a cooking course and would plan elaborate menus. I would shop for what he needed and be the helper while he cooked. You'd never have guessed we were talking about divorce a few months prior.

To this day, I think about that point in our lives. I vividly remember an experience in that house where Alexander was playing in his tree cubby while Ajwad ploughed the veggie patch. I sat, just chit-chatting away with Ajwad about nothing. And in this moment, there was bliss. Total bliss. I can touch it and feel it to this day. And it breaks my heart. Not because of me, but because of the stable life I could have given Alexander.

Our son adored us both. These really were happy times. We were good parents and finally had enough money after living on so little for so long. I can still remember the time of day I would look forward to Ajwad coming home from work. Even though we didn't have much in common intellectually, we were still good mates.

On a simple, homemaking level, our life was perfect. More

than perfect, really. As it was however, the truth kept creeping back and getting in the way, of this domestic bliss. I wanted more. I wanted love. I wanted my fairy-tale ending. I felt I had settled with Ajwad. And this is something that I consistently reminded myself of. Eventually, I began to pull away and became mean. I had to create some sort of justification for leaving.

Ajwad retaliated by becoming threatening. Our fights began to seethe with something that had been building in us both for years. How we had settled. How different our lives could have been. We, of course, loved Alexander dearly, but this wasn't about our son. This was about the decisions we had made and what our lives had become because of them.

"Don't push me," Ajwad would say as I spat poison from my tongue.

"Or what?" I would say as I stuck my nose right in his face to show him that no one scared me.

In those moments, I was a raving bitch. Fighting with words that shot like arrows. Words can be violent, and I knew where to hit. I felt stuck. Trapped. Enraged. Ajwad defended himself the only way he knew how, threatening to lash out if I didn't stop. We went on like this for months.

And then there was this one day that Ajwad started to threaten yet again. I reminded him mid-fight that he had promised not to threaten violence. We were trying to break our pattern.

He stopped for a second, looked at me, still full of anger but searching for a new way. He said, "Okay, then I'll burn your clothes."

We both began to laugh hysterically. Deep down, there was no real hate between us. We were two scared young adults who did their best to keep their baby in a culture saturated in shame. And now we both just really wanted and needed more.

But we continued to fight. Things didn't get better; they only seemed to slowly get worse. The day I made up my mind that the marriage absolutely must end, was the day Alexander jumped in between Ajwad and I when we were arguing.

"Don't hurt my mommy," Alexander said to his father. He could feel Ajwad's threatening energy.

This was all it took. I knew if we didn't separate, we would end up exactly like my parents. I would not see history repeat itself. I would not ruin my son's life because of my marital misery. It was this day I made up my mind. And this time, there was no going back.

I had begun to despise the trap of my marriage; it was like salt to a wound so deep it would never heal. All I knew was that I had to get out. The shame and pain overflowed, and it made me ugly. I had begun to wear it well. I became known as the bitch, and Ajwad, the nice guy. I did what I had to do and embraced the bitch I had become. I honoured her and allowed her to become my strength. I would strip myself of shame and instead wear my bitch badge with pride.

CAN'T YOU JUST HAVE AN AFFAIR AND GET IT OUT OF YOUR SYSTEM?

I'm not sure who I first told about getting a divorce. I do know, however, that my brother was my number one supporter. He lacked any judgement whatsoever. He was kind. For my brother, the breakup was simple.

"You deserve to be happy, sis," he said.

This was the day a new bond was forged between my brother and I. Where for years there had been strife, now there was only support. This bonding was crucial for my strength at this point of my life. I needed support. Needed someone who believed in me. My brother offered both.

It was my older sister who I thought would understand more than anyone. Instead, I received a lecture full of disappointment.

"How could you do this to your child?" she said to me. "Don't you think it's a bit selfish of you, Cindy?"

Didn't see that one coming! Wasn't she supposed to be the cool and hip older sister who broke all the rules?

And then there was Mum. "Can't you just have an affair and get it out of your system?" Mum never failed to surprise!

Ajwad wanted to stay married. He said I could do whatever I wanted as long as we maintained the façade of marriage. Really? Now, there was an offer that could have been worth taking! But when it came down to it, nothing less than getting a divorce was going to work for me. I could no longer live the lie. I needed my heart to be at peace.

Then there was Dad. He was sent to my house by Mum to talk some sense into me. This was something I found a bit strange. What were they trying to talk me into? They knew the truth. We got married because I was pregnant. It was all based on a lie. It honestly felt quite ridiculous to have my father trying to talk me into staying in a marriage based on a social pretense. And all my inner-child could think was, *but Daddy, don't you want more for me?* It seemed however, that the days of my inner-child were over. It was time to toughen up and stand strong in my truth.

So this is exactly what I began to do. My tolerance for letting others shame me for having a child was, by now, at almost zero. I had stripped myself of shame, and I would no longer play the game. I had all the arguments, and I wasn't afraid to use them.

I had built my case, ready for anyone who tried to challenge my decision. *A murderer kills and gets out of jail eventually. What was my sin? Giving life? I don't deserve to be in jail when I didn't do anything wrong!*

I was steadfast. There was no way I was going to back down.

Mum threw guilt at me. "After all we have done to support you and your marriage," she said. "If we knew you were going to get divorced, we may not have invested so much."

Thanks, Mum!

I wondered if Mum resented me for having the strength to leave. For standing for what I believed in and not taking back my decision. It was hard for her to be with my choice. I was resolute in leaving Ajwad, where for so many years she had lived resenting her marriage to my father.

I yearned for my parents to be by my side! But I was alone. Again. And the extended family didn't make things much easier. They were cruel. One of my uncles ignored me in his home, but paid enough attention to let me know he didn't want me socialising with his daughters, lest I infect them.

There truly was little support, aside from my brother. Others pointed out that if I loved my son, I would not leave. It hurt. Some would go on and on about what a nice guy Ajwad was. Telling me how they thought we were the 'perfect couple.' It felt like everyone was against me. I wondered if I was meant to feel this alone for the rest of my life. It honestly took all the strength I had to stand my ground.

DISOWNED AND RE-OWNED

Mum stopped talking to me.

I was crushed by this. I may have put up a strong front, but I still needed my mother. I was devastated. So much so that I went to see a counsellor at university. It was my first time. He was so blasé about the whole thing! He looked me straight in the eye.

"How old are you, Cindy?" he asked.

"Twenty-five," I told him.

"So what has this got to do with what your parents think?" he asked, so incredibly matter-of-factly. It was exactly what I needed. "You know," he went on to tell me, "in your culture it's normal for parents to pretend socially that they disapprove so they aren't judged by the community."

I was so disappointed. What about me and what I was going through? And while part of me didn't want to believe him, I would soon find this to be exactly how things played out.

I was now the hottest topic in my family. They judged me. They judged my parents. An endless cycle of guilt and judgement. The shame that accompanied all of it. I couldn't take it anymore. Damned if I would continue to feel shamed because of the lie I was living.

I was no longer willing to live this lie and planned on telling the truth about why I got married in the first place. I was no longer willing to be made out to be the bitch, while they all thought Ajwad was the nice guy and questioned how I could possibly do this to him. The whole charade was beginning to make me sick.

So I stood my ground. And to my surprise, everything started to turn around, just as my therapist at university told me it would. Mum and my aunties were now on my side. It was fascinating. I had the support I needed. *Why should she have to suffer like we have?* The conversation amongst them turned supportive. *Good on her*, they would now say when conversation turned my way.

I was not only the first female cousin amongst all forty cousins to get pregnant before marriage, but I was also the first one to get a divorce. Scandalous and unheard of.

One of my cousins called with support one day.

"How are you coping?" she asked. "Cindy, it must be so hard!" I was taken aback.

It was the first time someone had acknowledged that what I was going through might be a bit difficult, to say the least. I had little energy to put into feeling sorry for myself, however. I needed all the energy I could get just to follow through with what I was doing. I will never forget this extension of kindness, though.

I began to learn what it was like to have real relationships, where you don't need to keep up the façade. But living an authentic life takes work. I wasn't yet quite sure how to go about it. There were still many layers to peel away.

I WILL NOT TAKE HIM AWAY FROM YOU

Ajwad and I separated, but for the first few months we continued to live in the same house. Strangely, and completely unexpectedly, Ajwad and I became good friends during this time. I will never forget the day he came home and told me how happy he was. And who knows why? Maybe it was the taste of truth. Finally, the freedom and choice to really do whatever he wanted.

But it wasn't always so smooth. Ajwad wasn't always this happy. He would worry I would take Alexander away from him. He had heard stories from his family about the 'Western' women who take their children and never let the father see them. At one point, Ajwad looked truly depressed about the whole divorce thing. I was worried about him.

"You need your family," I told him. "I can't support you through this, Ajwad. You need to go see your family, and you should take Alexander with you."

And that's all it took. Off they went. Ajwad and Alexander on their way back to Lebanon. People would ask me how I could let Ajwad take our son with him. *What if he takes him away from you?* they asked, as if my situation was really any of their business to begin with.

But I just knew Ajwad wouldn't play that card.

All I knew was that he was hurting, and he needed a family of his own to support him. We were both hurting in our own way, though my newfound freedom helped me push down any pain I might have been feeling. I also knew I would never threaten Ajwad with not seeing his son, and he knew this. There are certain things that you just know. And between Ajwad and I, this was one of them. And I explicitly promised that I wouldn't.

For as much as Ajwad and I were making do in the first months following our separation, his family was far from impressed. They adored and fussed over Alexander, who was two-and-half, but I was something to despise. From Ajwad's family's point of view, their son had saved me my dignity by marrying me in the first place. And now I was trashing his. Fair enough. These days, I can see it from their perspective.

Despite his trip to Lebanon, when Ajwad returned, he was still lost, and living in the same house as a separated couple was difficult. I learnt that getting separated doesn't happen quite as easily as it does in the movies. Running two households was quite an expensive undertaking.

Ajwad was finding it hard to figure out what to do with his life, so he decided to go to the U.S. to spend time with his brother. There was a dream in Ajwad that had never died, a dream that he and his brother would one day work together. Ajwad was trying to realise his dreams, and I believed that he should follow them. But the reality was that he could not easily work and live in the U.S., and having a child you couldn't live without was never written into the equation of Ajwad's

American dream. He adored Alexander, which turned into a bitter inner struggle between wanting and needing to be close to him and wanting to be close to his family. He spent two months in the U.S. and then returned home, realising that he needed to be close to his son. The time had finally come to live in separate homes and to formalise our divorce.

ADJUSTING TO LIFE ALONE

In my desperation to put my marriage behind me as soon as possible, I lacked compassion. I was looking at the situation through a practical lens rather than a loving one.

I suppose I was compassionate enough at times. I did help Ajwad find a flat and help move him in. But then my anger would get the best of me, and I would inform him that it was he that should be inconvenienced, not me. I was the mother, which meant I should come first. Some weird programming that in hindsight is quite embarrassing.

We did it, though. We moved forward with separating our lives. Anyone who saw Ajwad and I interacting from the outside was at a loss as to why we were even getting a divorce. This was all while horror stories were coming out on the news about divorced parents handing over children at police stations. Ajwad and I were suddenly the ideal divorced couple.

Eventually, my family adjusted and was amazing throughout the entire process. They were once again by my side. And they still treated Ajwad like he was part of the family. While this annoyed me because it made me feel married still, other times I was grateful, seeing as he was the father of my child. Things could have been a lot worse. For not knowing what we were doing, I think Ajwad and I did a very good job. We had no one to model ourselves after, so we muddled on through with good intentions. I'm not only sad about the impact this all had on my son, but also about the impact it had on Ajwad and myself.

So there I was, desperate to have my freedom, and I finally got it. This is why the loneliness I experienced without Ajwad came as such a shock. I literally had no idea what to do with myself. I went from primary caretaker having Alexander every single day of my life, to this huge void of suddenly having a whole weekend to myself.

I couldn't believe how lost I felt. I thought I would immediately enjoy it, but it took some time to adjust. Eventually, it was great to have space to study on the weekends and do my own thing. But, my God, the first few months were difficult. It was like I had to reconstruct my entire life. This wasn't something I had taken into consideration.

The upside of things was that Alexander and his dad now spent more time together. Ajwad was amazing with Alexander. Not that he always wasn't, but as a single dad, Ajwad's true colours really did shine through. I never worried about the well-being of Alexander when he was with his father. Didn't worry if he was going to be fed properly or bathed and clothed in the right way. Ajwad was such a lovely homemaker in fact, that I began to enjoy the times I would drop by his place. We were learning how to remain a family despite being separated. I refused to relate to Alexander as having a broken home, so I took on teaching him that he had multiple homes where he was loved.

TAKING THINGS A BIT TOO FAR

Things eventually began to become too much for me. Ajwad had seriously hit rock bottom and was reacting poorly to our separation. Just as I thought things were going so well. I knew Ajwad was hurting, but so was I. No matter what I did, be it good or bad, this drama seemed to never end. All I knew at this point in my life was that I needed a break. An escape from the drama, an escape from the gossip. And perhaps most importantly, I needed to find an escape from the internal confusion and very familiar feeling of being lost that had come back in full force since becoming a single woman again. My three years of marriage had pushed it down, but now there was nowhere for me to hide.

I decided I would apply to go to Paris on exchange to finish my final semester in my degree. The perfect escape. I was accepted. Was I making the right decision? I didn't dare stop long enough to think about it. I had no tools to confront what I was dealing with. I just needed out. And I once again made up my mind that I would simply do whatever the hell I wanted, especially when making my plans for escape masked any pain I might be feeling.

I ended my lease on the house I was renting. I organised for my parents to pick up my parenting days. Where Alexander was concerned, Ajwad would do the rest. What I didn't bargain for was just how long four months away would feel like.

While Paris sounded like such a great idea, when it came down to it, the whole thing only increased my sense of feeling all alone in the world. And no one could have prepared me for the emptiness I would feel being without my child. God, yes, I needed a break, but back then, four months was an eternity. Not just for me, but for little Alexander as well. If I could do it all over, I would never leave my four-year-old like that.

I was miserable the entire time I was in Paris. No one told me how incomplete I would feel without my child. There was no Skype back then, no cell phones. International calls were so damn expensive, which all made the contact I had with Alexander very, very little. And while I seriously didn't have a good time while I was there, I was still too ashamed to go home early. I had heard of people who blamed their horrible life on falling pregnant. I was determined not to be one of them. I promised myself I would never let my son be an excuse for not living a great life. I would never let Alexander become the reason I stopped doing the things I wanted to do. I would never be the mother who was a martyr, blaming her child because she didn't get the life she wanted.

Turns out, I may have taken this a bit too far.

PLAYING WITH FIRE

The year I was planning my exchange trip to Paris, I decided I would add in a side trip to Lebanon. In preparation for this trip, I thought it might be nice to make some new friends. Somehow, I found a list of Lebanese on an Internet website and decided to connect with them. This, mind you, was the very early days of the Internet. Back then it was nothing like it is today.

There were no pictures of these people I was befriending. They were mostly my age, a mixture of both men and women. I hadn't been back to Lebanon in five years, and I knew a lot had changed. I wanted to expand my horizons, not be stuck in the same old village life with which I was so familiar. I ended up writing to two men for almost a year, and as time went by, we began to become friends. This is long before any form of social media, and it was something new and exciting. I planned on meeting both these men when I arrived in Lebanon for my detour trip.

I had complained to one of these email pals about how difficult I found it to socialise in Paris. It was so boring! And it was the dead of winter, which didn't help things at all. Not only was I homesick and missing my son terribly, I was incredibly lonely. Again! My email friend assured me I wouldn't be bored in Lebanon. It was a place to have fun! He promised to take me out the moment I arrived.

I had no expectations and was honestly just happy with this lovely friendship that had blossomed. It would also be nice to have someone show me around Beirut. True to his word, the evening I arrived in Lebanon, he came to my parents' home in the village to pick me up. When I opened the door, I clearly remember my breath catching in my throat. He wasn't supposed to be so handsome, so well dressed, and with such a strong presence.

Every day spent together only brought us closer. We began spending as much time together as possible on my short, two-week stay. There was a magic between us. A 'this only happens in the movies' kind of feeling. I couldn't get enough of him. It was the perfect escape from how I was feeling.

Despite the chemistry, however, there was a big cultural divide between us. I had Lebanese parents and knew how they thought. Being a single mum, recently separated, was a huge cultural *faux-pas*, and was not going to go over well with his family. I joked about it. We both did, pretending all this was just some holiday romance. But we both knew our feelings were growing deeper.

Eventually, it came time to leave. He wanted me to stay. As much as I wanted to do so, I couldn't see any real future for us. Not to mention, I desperately missed Alexander and needed to return home to him. Goodbyes were said, and after a two-week whirlwind romance, I returned to Australia. The emails continued, however. *I still want you,* he would write. *I still miss you.* And as much as I knew it wouldn't work, it was still something. I wasn't ready for the fantasy to end. So when the dreaded day came that he told me he had been talking to his mother about me, I already knew what was coming next. He let me know how he felt society would never accept our relationship. I was crushed. Damaged goods.

Who better to comfort me in a crisis than Mum? I turned to her, climbing into bed with her one morning. What was with me and climbing into bed with Mum when I was having a crisis? I told her that this was the first time I ever regretted keeping my baby and getting married. My heart was broken. And as much as I felt that I was betraying Alexander for thinking such thoughts, I really believed I was damaged goods. Not only in my eyes, but in those of a Lebanese mother. I would never get the fairy-tale romance of which I had always secretly dreamt.

I compared every man to him for years. But nothing compared. And then, although it took a while, I began to grow up. I learnt the difference between fantasy and reality. Had I more self-esteem, a healthier relationship with my father, or even just a little more experience, I might not have played the game we did. I was the one who seduced him. I knew I was playing with fire. It was how I filled the empty void that always seemed to hang around, like a constant fog.

When it came down to it however, I was still a sucker for good looks, great kissing, intelligence, ambition, and a great pair of shoes! Any time I would begin to feel that kind of connection with another man, however, I would pull back. Never did I want to feel the pain of such rejection again.

LIVING AN AUTHENTIC LIFE

Having finished my degree, I returned to my job that was still waiting for me. I appreciated the security, but this time, work left me feeling dead. I told Mum that I wanted to leave my job. "Do you think it is wise to leave your job given that you don't have a husband?" she asked. On the one hand, Mum was Miss Progressive. Then, out of nowhere these old-fashioned notions would spill out of her mouth, flooring me. My parents wanted security for me, and having a stable job provided that. I needed more. So despite my fear, I left with nothing solid to go to. My personal integrity had to come first. I had sold out on myself before with dire consequences. This time, I had to have the courage to live a more authentic life.

I had started my Masters degree and reasoned that studying full-time would be great. It would give me more time with Alexander. My mentor and my supervisors also suggested that I should upgrade to a PhD and that I should apply for a scholarship. So I did both. With this great support, I was accepted into my PhD program and granted a scholarship. The universe had provided. Life with Alexander was blissful during my student years. I felt like a good mother, desperately wanting to make up for ever leaving him for so long.

HIGH OCTANE

I am woman
I am invincible
I am exhausted

"I must be overtired', Buttercup managed. 'The excitement and all."
"Rest then", her mother cautioned. "Terrible things can happen when you're overtired. I was overtired the night your father proposed."

—William Goldman

"I'm tired."
"Sleep."
"No, you don't understand."

— Anonymous

PEACE AND DESERT WINDS

After eighteen months doing my PhD, I decided to take a one-month break. It was good timing. I felt restless yet again. So I returned to Lebanon, this time with Alexander. He would spend some time with his father's family whilst I backpacked around Syria, Jordan, and Egypt. Part of my rebellion was to not let the fact that I was a woman stop me from doing whatever I wanted. I didn't tell my parents, knowing they would put the fear of God in me.

I arrived in Syria by bus. There were no women in the streets, and the men undressed me with their eyes. How I longed to be covered from head to toe! I'd come with no plan. No hotel was booked, nor did I have an itinerary to follow. Just me and my *Lonely Planet* travel guide in hand. I yearned to just go with the flow.

I arrived in Aleppo and found a small guest house that came highly recommended by my travel guide. The part that attracted me to it the most was that it was run by a Lebanese woman named Olga, who was quick to inform me that her impeccable home was full for the evening. I quickly moved into seduction mode and hoped it would work, even on this sixty-year-old woman.

"My grandmother's name is Olga," I gushed when she told

me her name. "And so is mine!" Finally putting the Olga part of my name to good use.

She wasn't exactly the warm and fuzzy kind, but I knew a cord had been struck. I just hoped that slipping in my Lebaneseness and all would somehow get me a bed for the night. Her home made me feel safe. Thankfully, my strategy worked in my favour. Madame Olga had a tour guide who had arrived before me sleep on the lounge room couch, and I was moved into his lovely room for the night. The whole house oozed the impeccability and cleanliness one could count on from any self-respecting Lebanese homemaker. A backpacker's dream.

If there was any country that provided an authentic cultural experience, it was Syria. Aleppo, in particular, served up authenticity on a platter. Syria had a ban on anything Western in order to preserve its culture. No internet. No mobile phones. There was no Gap, no United Colours of Benetton, no McDonald's, no nothing. There wasn't even a single sign in English. There were men still hanging out with their donkeys on the streets! At the markets, each stall sold only one item. And while there may have been what appeared to be little consumer choice, everything you needed was still available. Somehow, this felt peaceful. I was so grateful for this anti-Western ban. I saw wisdom in it, but we all know what can happen when choice is taken from the people.

I woke up one morning to find Madame Olga taking full charge of my trip. She was mortified that I was travelling alone. She arranged for me to join an American tourist who was being taken for a private, off-the-beaten-track tour with a Syrian tour guide whom she knew personally. This way, she could be certain I would be safe. That's how this part of the world is. People look after you. And of course, this off-the-beaten-track tour was an offer I could not resist.

So that was that. I had myself a free tour around Syria. From Aleppo to Hama, then to Homs. From Homs we went deep into the Syrian Desert to Palmyra. For some strange reason, the desert gave me deep comfort. Peace. Seeing the Bedouins with their goats was so beautiful it almost didn't feel real. I wondered, though, how these people felt about their lives, spent in the middle of the desert. Palmyra was like a scene out of a movie, with the desert winds howling throughout the amazing ruins. Here, in the middle of nowhere, I felt right at home. There was a strange and unexpected pull to stay.

I only allowed these thoughts a second of headspace as they were foreign to me, and no match for the identity I had fantasised myself into. I didn't understand what I was feeling or why. This was a point in my life where I was trying desperately to be interesting and glamorous, yet I had such a profound sense of being at home there, where the desert was magic. From Palmyra we headed to Damascus, where I parted ways with my tour guide. I found myself a service taxi and made my way to Jordan.

The drive from Syria to Jordan literally felt like I was in a movie about Jesus or Moses. The rock formations took my breath away. Arriving at Petra, I was equally awed by the natural beauty. Next came Amman, the capital of Jordan, which was a bit like Lebanon. Not quite as cosmopolitan, but similar. I found a backpackers' haven that was full of foreigners. It was here I met a beautiful Armenian man. We hung out on the rooftop till 5:00 a.m., awed by the call to prayer.

I will never forget what he said to me as I shared with him my guilt for leaving Alexander in Lebanon with his grandmother and aunties so I could take this trip. God only knows what they thought of me, but I both did and didn't care. I obviously didn't care enough not to travel.

"You know the thing about guilt?" he said.

"What's that?" I asked, prepared for some life changing words of wisdom.

"It's such a waste of time."

There are some things, some moments, that stay with you always.

Although it felt as if I could stay in his gorgeous Armenian arms forever, I continued south. I arrived in Aqaba, and as nice as this port city on the Red Sea was, it felt a bit empty, lonely and devoid of soul. So I made my way back to the desert, this time Wadi Rum, the Valley of Rome, a location made famous by the movie *Lawrence of Arabia* in 1962. There, I spent a night camping under the stars.

Cairo came next, and with it came all the chaos and noise you could imagine. Gypsies on the street. Music. Vibrant colour and deliciously foreign smells. I immediately fell in love with it. I wandered out, captivated by the foreign world that surrounded me. I found myself in a perfumery, seduced by the Egyptian smells. I met a local man who offered to show me around. We visited the pyramids, which broke my heart. They were right on the edge of the city, though it looked like the edge of the slums. Nothing like the pictures you see.

It was such a disappointment.

My new friend however, knew exactly how to cheer me up. He offered to take me to his village, and of course, I accepted. Off we went. Oh, what a trip! We arrived in his village, and as we walked the streets together I felt like a superstar! All the children ran after us, repeatedly using the four words of English they knew: *Hello, how are you?* There was a fifteen-year-old girl breastfeeding her baby in one arm while doing her homework with her other hand. In the background, you could see three small pyramids. The sun was setting behind them. It was utterly surreal. The village felt amazing.

While I had felt at home all the way along my trip, the feeling was stronger here in this little village with pyramids in the background. I was then invited to dinner by my host. It was prepared by his mother, a humble woman who served us a lovely meal on a huge tray made of discoloured bronze. I sat on the floor with him, his mother, and his sister-in-law (whose husband had recently died). Before I knew it, my little tour was over, and a few hours later I was safely back in my guest house. I was grateful for my chance encounters on this trip and the hospitality they showed me. It made the travel risks I took worthwhile.

My entire trip only took two weeks. High speed and saturated in adventure. Looking back, though, I wish I would have known how to slow it down. I rushed through, not daring to slow down, lest I feel that emptiness inside. Now, this part of the world is nowhere near safe to go. At least I got to see those countries in their happier days, which is something I will forever hold close to my heart.

UNDERNEATH THE SURFACE

Despite my defiant ways, the need to make my parents proud of me was always underneath the surface. There was a guilt that ran the show. Guilt about having brought shame to the family. The decision to make my parents proud, however, only reinforced my feelings of shame and failure, although not consciously. So day in, day out, as I set out to prove myself and redeem myself, my actions would simply reinforce my belief that I was damaged goods and shameful. I had finally gotten my way and was out of my marriage, but still felt the constant nag of discontent. And now there was no one left to blame.

This was a huge realisation for me. Maybe my unhappiness had nothing to do with my marriage. I really thought that if I was free of my marriage, my life would be wonderful. At least my life was now no longer a façade.

Despite completing my degree and progressing towards a PhD, living in a lovely flat, and having had many a travelling experience, I could not understand, for the life of me, why the joy from these accomplishments was so fleeting, lasting a few days at most. Now, all that was left was that dangling carrot. The elusive search that someday, one day, I would find a way to fill the hole I felt deep inside. But try as I did, I simply couldn't get the lasting fulfillment I was looking for.

TRANSFORMATION ENVY

Midway through my PhD I was introduced, through a friend, to the world of personal development and transformation. I began attending workshops where I learnt about creating my life rather than trying to fix or survive it. Up until then I lived my life as if something was wrong with me. I had been trying to build my life from a faulty foundation. I learnt that my fundamental life story was that I was damaged goods, unloved and alone. Living from this 'story' was the source of my unhappiness, not what my parents did or didn't do whilst I was growing up, not the fact that I got pregnant, married, and then divorced, and not that I was judged along the way. This kind of personal development was fast-paced, which suited my need for speed. Eventually, life began to take on new meaning. I took on the perspective that anything was possible for my life, with a vengeance. It was time to let go of my sad past. I began to take charge of my life as opposed to react to it or compensate for where I believed I had gone wrong.

I was also introduced to the concept of responsibility. The idea that we are always the source of our experience. It was my relationship to circumstances that held the greatest power. Meaning, how I interpreted the circumstances, not the circumstances themselves.

But for a long time I confused responsibility with self-blame and lacked compassion for myself. I had yet to learn the importance of feeling my feelings, so instead I rationalised them. I diminished my feelings down to hard facts and merely my interpretation on a particular situation, which was insufficient for real and lasting healing.

For a while, though, I felt invincible as I feasted on the world of personal empowerment. But in my arrogance I forgot that I was still a beginner. Confusing myself with an expert in this work was costly, damaging my relationships rather than creating closer connections, as was intended. This played out, mostly, in my relationship with my mother. I would get stuck in a cycle of insight and taking responsibility one day only to blame her the next. A love-hate relationship. Best friends one day, sworn enemies the next. It was hard for Mum to gauge which Cindy she would get on any given day. Trust eroded despite my efforts to be 'evolved.'

If I wasn't focusing on meeting some new goal I had created, I focused on having a breakthrough. The art of uncovering a personal blindspot in how I was behaving. With each challenge life threw at me, I simply worked harder at uncovering these blindspots that were potentially getting in the way of my invincibility. I was trained to welcome a 'breakdown', a state of not getting the results I wanted, be it an emotional state or a tangible goal. The term 'no breakdown, no breakthrough' further encouraged me to take on more challenges. If I wasn't experiencing any breakdowns, clearly I wasn't playing big enough in my life. This new way of living my life was exhilarating, at first. I felt like I was on a high for two straight years.

A few years on, I started developing my leadership. Leadership was a way of being, we were taught, not a title bestowed upon you from the outside by virtue of a job. Ghandi's 'be the change you want to see in the world' was the flavour of those days. We were encouraged to take the attention off ourselves and contribute to others and the world around us. Coaching was the medium of contribution. Specifically, transformational coaching—focusing on changing the way one sees oneself—which was how I received my training along the way. I fell in love with this medium. I loved being coached (sometimes!), as well as being a coach. When I focused on supporting someone else's transformation and breakthroughs, I, in turn, experienced my own transformation and breakthroughs. I felt for the first time in my life that I had found my calling.

It was the early days of coaching becoming a profession, and I rode the wave. I loved coaching so much that when I finally turned to it as a full-time profession, it was hard for me to believe that I could also be paid for it. Finally, a job that was not about survival or trying to prove myself. Coaching was a pure labour of love.

The benefits of my development extended to other relationships in my family. The conversations I was having with my brother became more authentic. I learnt about him and his childhood stories, and how he saw things. We shared our mutual pain and sadness for those difficult days, wishing they were different. We compared notes. Strangely, the things that had caused him pain had caused envy in me. A new intimacy and trust was formed.

Then came my relationship with Dad. Now with greater awareness, I realised that I had distanced myself from him as punishment for his failure in business and the impact it had had on our family and, in particular, my mother. I had silently taken her side in their arguments. I was also ashamed of Dad's ethnicity and lack of appropriateness at times. I began to see humour in his behaviour rather than embarrassment.

For his entire life, Dad wore Calvin Klein-like underwear. Even before they became fashionable. He went to sleep in them and walked around the house in them. Nudity was never seen as a bad thing in our home. So one day, when I had my friend sleeping over, Dad pranced down the stairs in his underwear. I'm sure he didn't expect us to be there, but he was quick.

"Don't worry, darling," he said to her in his strong accent, "I won't charge you for seeing my sexy body." With that, he laughed his head off and just kept going to the kitchen.

I was mortified. But my friend loved him. She found him hilarious.

Then there were the days of driving us to school in Lebanon. We picked up two other kids from the village and took them to school with us. Dad thought his machine gun-sounding farts were hilarious. I just wanted to disappear. He would not only break wind, he would break out in hysterical laughter, joking that they smelt like roses.

Finally, the shame around my father both came to the surface and loosened its grip, making way for me to gently let him know when he was going overboard without withdrawing my love. And in turn, he was able to hear me—well, on occasion at least.

I started to actively create opportunities to spend time with my father alone. I invited him out to lunch one day, to make it up to him for being unavailable on Father's Day, and had a huge insight. I had been having a relationship with my mother's opinion of Dad rather than my dad himself. Around that time, I got out of my parents' relationship and began to have my own relationship with each of them. I informed both of them that their relationship was their own private business, not mine, and stepped out of my 'little counsellor' role.

This was my family. And during this time, I started to accept it for what it was. I'm not saying one day everything was suddenly fine. My acceptance would fluctuate one day to the next.

During these years I spent working on myself, which were by no means easy, I oscillated between being driven by external accomplishments to being driven to have a breakthrough. If I saw someone else glowing from their own personal insight and transformation, it would propel me to work deeper and harder on myself. Transformation envy. Arrogance. We were warned about it. After all, *today's transformation is tomorrow's ego trip*. And God knew my ego was alive and well.

When my family felt they needed to point something out to me, though, I would get very intellectual in my arguments with them. Very 'transformed', even self-righteous and superior. Oh, how I exhausted them with my intellect! It was the only way I was able to keep down the pain and shame I had yet to allow myself to feel fully.

I will always consider these years some of the most transformative of my life. What I learnt was helpful in so many ways. I took charge of my life. I truly started to believe I could create anything. I began to feel my power. And I revelled in it. But it had its limits.

LITTLE HOUSE ON THE PRAIRIE

Around my thirtieth birthday, Mum had organised a small day trip for the two of us. We were going to the country to look at buying a home. Together. I would live in it, and my parents would have some capital in it. Not that I ever had any fantasies about living in the country. I'd have preferred Melbourne, but there was simply no way I could afford a house there. So I went with it.

The idea was to go check out houses for sale. When we arrived at the real estate agent's office, he told us about a piece of land that was up for auction that very afternoon. He suggested it wouldn't hurt to just take a look. Just to be fair to Mum, I agreed to take a look at the property. I had no interest in land and had no time to build a house. When we arrived late to the auction after getting lost in the forest, the real estate agent suggested we have a look around. Mum and I walked to the top of the hill, wind blowing gently around us. The grass swayed beautifully in the breeze, and there was a dam that was full to the brim with water.

Then I turned around and saw the view. And that was it. In a nanosecond, I knew I had to have this piece of land. It was magical. A three hundred-degree view of the Mount Macedon Ranges. It stirred memories of watching Little House on the

Prairie, when the girls would run through the grass in the countryside. It reminded me a bit of Lebanon as well, living with the privilege of waking up each day to a stunning view. It wasn't the Mediterranean, but it was Australia. There were kangaroos, and it was abound with Australian authenticity.

And as fate would have it, we were the only ones bidding that day. By two in the afternoon, I was a certified property owner. And as a thirtieth birthday present, Mum allowed me to own the land outright, given that I could actually afford it. My scrimping and saving for years, despite being a single mother, was paying off. My parents loaned me the last bit of money I needed, and that was that. I wouldn't have been able to purchase a parking space in Melbourne for the price of this gorgeous ten acres of land.

I finally felt connected to Australia.

SAVING THE WORLD

A couple of years later, I completed my PhD. Now that I had worked so hard on transforming myself, I thought it was time I took on transforming the world!

Peace in the Middle East!

That would keep me busy.

I took on the burden of what was happening in Lebanon like it was mine to carry. I remember thinking to myself that if everyone in the world learnt to stop blaming and took responsibility instead, perhaps war would one day be resolved. How I underestimated the depths of the wounds I would later see.

I had begun creating a documentary called *An Interview With My People*. I wanted to form my own views, first-hand, about the war in Lebanon rather than be influenced by the views that circulated in conversations when I was growing up. I had a small team that planned on coming to Lebanon with me to make this documentary. It was about understanding the war and life in Lebanon from the perspective of everyday people. The Iraq War broke out soon after, however, and the Australian government put out alerts that people should not travel anywhere in the Middle East. Everyone pulled out, and I was crushed. But I went anyway.

I was determined to go and learn about all the things I didn't understand. And along the way, I met many people who told me their stories. These stories, however, horrified me. I became versed in how movements had started. It was the youth, in their late-twenties and early-thirties, that led the way. It started with graffiti on walls that later grew into more vocal activities. Along the way these activists were sometimes kidnapped and beaten, their families never knowing if they would come home alive. I was unprepared for the impact listening to these stories would have on me.

I met a reporter who took me to the Palestinian refugee camps. And just because I thought my nine-year-old son needed to see the world as it really was, I took him with me. At one point, we were walking up the stairs of one of the buildings in the refugee camps as a woman came storming up beside us, completely distraught about not being able to get her husband the medication he desperately needed.

In her distress, she accidently pushed Alexander out of the way. He was devastated, and I questioned myself about exposing him to this world. There was something else, however, that told me sheltering our children wasn't necessarily the best thing either.

I then met a young woman my age, who couldn't have been older than thirty. She told me about the wars that broke out within the refugee camps, and how her brother had died in her arms. She took me to see the graves. I walked into a room, unaware that the graves were all on the ground. I accidently stepped on one, which is a huge disrespect for those buried. It was Alexander who pulled me off, his awareness much more in tune than my own.

I wondered if this woman would be up for grabbing a coffee with me in Beirut, but was informed by the reporter who had brought me there that she had probably never left the refugee camp. How foolish I felt! The entrenchment of my Australian mind! It was difficult for me to digest the reality of what life in a refugee camp really was. What I did know was that it was filthy. And smelled horribly. Strangely, I was expecting tents, but instead they lived in buildings.

"If you had a chance to go and live in another country, would you go?" I asked the young woman who had so graciously shown us around. "If you knew it would be safe?"

"Palestine is our home," she replied without a moment's hesitation. "We will never give up on it." What followed was something about being willing to have it cost their blood.

I was stunned. She wasn't born in Palestine, but the fight for the Palestinians to one day return 'home' to what was now called Israel, was in her veins, and she would never give up.

We then went to visit another camp, which almost seemed upmarket compared to the camp I had just visited. I spoke to young boys who were fourteen-years-old who told me they needed to get an education. That they needed to learn how to speak in a way that made others respect the Palestinian people. Thankfully, a little bit of hope was restored.

It was during this visit I learnt of something else that deeply saddened me. There was a problem arising with babies being born with deformities. Relations of the mother and father it seemed, were too close. There was one child lying on a bed, unable to walk because of his disability. Others that faired luckier were left with cleft palates or harelips. I didn't want to imagine the mental ramifications a problem such as this would cause.

I met a doctor who did volunteer work at another refugee camp who agreed to take me with him. Here, there were Palestinians, Syrians, and a host of other displaced refugees with no papers, no identification. Essentially, they were trapped there. When I arrived, a group of men and women were sitting around on a carpet having mint tea. It was such a lovely sight, but the pain in their eyes was hard to miss. Children played basketball with a hoop created by a chair with no bottom. The children didn't have much, but at least they looked happy.

The doctor informed me about the corruption of the Non-Governmental Organisations (NGOs) and how little money gets to the people who need it. He told me of the depression that plagued many of the residents. He wondered aloud if there were better skills to offer the children than the focus on traditional education. Practical skills they would need. Skills to support them to live in the confines of a refugee camp.

I was a bit numb by this point, and not much more got in. One thing however, became crystal clear. Transformation was one way to shift the mindset of war, but what about the deep trauma that wasn't handled? What if basic food needs were not met? Basic medicinal needs not provided? If the possibility of a future wasn't available, how was anything ever going to change?

I managed to get an interview with the then ex-army general, who was in exile in Paris. I also bargained with Alexander. Told him I would take him with me to meet my French university friends if he would forgive me for leaving him when he was four. He was now nine. I was desperate to make up for where I believed I had failed at being a mother. And I thought some maternal manipulation might work.

Paris turned out to be the most perfect trip ever. One of my friends arranged for us to have a suite at the Sofitel Paris le Faubourg for only fifty euros a night. She worked there. When we arrived, she greeted us with four Parisian chocolate eclairs, knowing how much I absolutely loved them.

The first two I ate whilst Alexander slept. And though I knew it was awful of me, I polished off the last two before he woke. He was understandably devastated. How could I be so thoughtless as to not even leave him one? I tried to reason with him, saying we could just go out and get more. We were in Paris, after all. There was a patisserie on every corner. But his feelings were hurt nonetheless. Today, we still get quite a laugh at what a 'not' mother I could sometimes be.

My other university friend lived on a boat on the River Seine. It felt like I was having a mini reunion. We hung out on the boat and ate, we picnicked at Versailles, and roamed around taking pictures of Moulin Rouge and Notre Dame. We had our portraits painted at Montmartre. That trip to Paris was one of the best Alexander and I ever had together.

No further inspiration came from my meeting with the army general. It was clear to him that the only solution was to get the Palestinians out of Lebanon but was not explicit on exactly how. Given what I had seen in the refugee camps, I was not optimistic much would change any time soon. Not without the shedding of more innocent blood.

My trip to Lebanon had me question whether a purely

transformational approach would make the difference required to bring peace to such a war-torn country. Yes, taking responsibility is always important, but what of the deep emotional wounding that resulted from years of brutal war? I hadn't taken that into consideration. I couldn't help but wonder how many therapists it would take to heal an entire nation. I left Lebanon filled with a deep despondency. Guilty for wanting to run away. I felt dark inside, unsure about my place in the world. Sad for my birth country. I went from believing that I could change the world to being completely resigned about any hope of peace in the Middle East.

In the midst of my anguish, there was only one thing that made any sense to me. First, I needed to take responsibility. If I was serious about peace, I would need to start with myself. I needed to find my own inner peace before I could make any difference in the world. I needed to own how I would silently and emotionally wage war on those who hurt me. War is not always waged with guns. I had waged it with a simple roll of the eye, killing someone's spirit or cutting off my love for them. Being committed to peace began to take on a whole new meaning.

And so began a new journey toward deeper healing. At times, it was a journey I wished I had never started.

HOME

Given I was now in my early thirties, my cultural programming began to warn me not to get left on the shelf. This programming left little room for discernment. And given my lack of awareness of this deep cultural programming, I went along with the advances of the first man willing to take me seriously. He was seventeen years older than me and could handle my temperamental ways. I may have been working on myself, but I was still a handful as a woman with a strong mind of my own. Once again, however, I failed to tune into my feelings and needs. I didn't have the skills for this yet. So I allowed myself to get swept up into this relationship only to realise that despite our mutual love of personal development, we had little else in common. We couldn't even align on taking a holiday together, let alone what to have for dinner. I may have been a handful, but at fifty, he was set in his ways, which bored me. But by then, we were engaged. I called Dad one day. "Dad, I'm so unhappy."

"Pack your bags and come home," he said. So I did.

That year, I moved house six times. I was everywhere, but going nowhere. Given my relationship breakup and my many years of restlessness, I kept uprooting myself. If I wasn't moving house, I was planning an extended trip overseas. And because I never had a home base to come back to, I would often feel homeless. It was exhausting starting over each time. I began to desperately crave my own home. I had my own piece of land. Now it was time to build *my own* home. I couldn't keep living the way I was. I yearned for the safety a home would provide.

Given my passion for personal development and coaching, I had decided to become a professionally certified coach. To avoid putting pressure on myself, I initially took this new profession on as a hobby whilst completing my PhD, and with time, my client base grew, but it had yet to provide me with a stable income. In addition to this, the banks weren't thrilled about ten acres in the middle of nowhere as security for the loan I was asking for, but eventually I was able to find one willing bank. And, of course, I didn't want any old home. I wanted a statement, no matter how small it was. There weren't many architects who were interested in building a small, low-cost home that had architectural flair. This was before tiny homes were all the rage.

The architects who finally accepted the brief were amazing. A husband and wife team who were some of the most creative people I'd ever met. Working with them to design my home was the best project I had ever taken on.

Whilst our new home was being built, Alexander and I moved into a new rental home and were in bliss. It was right around the corner from his father's house, and he was able to come and go between the two houses as he pleased. We had the most wonderful pyjama days, just lazing around the house on Saturdays, not doing much of anything.

And although it wasn't the sexiest part of town, I could afford it, and for now it felt like home. It felt safe. It's the unsexy parts of my life that have often felt the most satisfying. Again, something I was blind to at the time.

Aside from the amazing architects, I found a lovely builder who began to build my dream into reality. It seemed that I was going to be able to build this home on my modest budget after all! Everyone warned me I was heading for a nightmare, though. Apparently, problems arise when building a house and budgets always blow out. Not in my case. I had the reverse experience. Everything worked out perfectly with the budget I had. I loved my home. Sadly, I barely got to live in it as my career took off.

NEW YORK, NEW YORK

With my home now underway, it was time to transform my financial situation. I needed a job that paid well. I was exhausted from worrying about money and my financial security all the time.

I got a job interview for a role as a management consultant with a company that focused on organisational transformation. I was completely in sync with their vision as a business and the difference they were committed to making. So much so that I choked on my tears of joy during my interview. Not the smoothest move, but I couldn't help myself. And I couldn't believe my luck. They liked my emotional commitment and hired me within days. Overnight, I was making a comfortable salary. I went from what felt like an income of a pittance to the ability to afford much more than I ever had. It might as well have been a million dollars. It is all relative after all.

Although I was in the middle of building my house, my new job—consulting for construction and mining industries—made it possible for me not to lose my mind about taking on debt. This new position required a lot of travel, and seeing as Ajwad had asked to have Alexander full-time—I had been the full-time parent up until this point—I would have the freedom to do so. I figured it would be good for Alexander, who was now twelve, to spend more time with his father. So I was able to accept a job that demanded much of my time away. I thought it was the job of a lifetime. And my parents were so proud. I truly felt like I was recovering from my years of being seen as damaged goods.

I had to fly to Stamford, Connecticut in the U.S. to begin training. I was picked up by a limo at the airport in New York and taken to stay the night at the Helmsley. How satisfying to my ever-inflating ego this was! What else signifies 'making it' more than travelling to New York and being picked up in a limo? I was in heaven.

New York certainly lived up to its reputation. It was awash with style, oozing money and class everywhere I turned. I'd never seen men dressed better than women! Melbourne was a sleepy village by comparison! Why hadn't this been my first travel destination when I was nineteen? Why was my life always so back to front?

I was convinced that this was 'the life.' My love affair with the idea of success began to actualise. I was intoxicated with ambition, drive, and speed. However, I confused being inspired with being driven. I went from 'I ruined my life' to 'I can do anything.' Have money, a home, a career, sexy clothes. Have it all!

Yes, this is exactly what they told us women. That we could have it all. But what they were referring to was external accomplishment, not inner peace. They never told us that the pursuit of external accomplishment came at a cost. Not just to ourselves, either.

And though I was awash with fear and anxiety about being

able to do a good job in this new position, I got busy very quickly. It was at the height of the mining boom, so work was abundant, and I was in demand. Before too long I was working at full-capacity. Every consultant's dream. The more I worked, the more work I was asked to do. It was heroin for my ego.

THE CRACKS

With all the success I was experiencing, missing the early signposts of anxiety was easy. It crept in slowly, but I didn't recognise it as anxiety. I simply felt inadequate. As good as I was with one-on-one coaching, the fear would kick in when I had to face a room full of people. Our clients were executives, and I, barely just a mother.

Because I had such an air of confidence, few people picked up on the fact that I was terrified to speak in front of a room. Oftentimes, even *I* didn't. There were the occasions, however, where I would completely clam up when I knew I couldn't escape having to face a room full of 'important' people.

Luckily, on the few occasions when I would freeze in front of clients, I would be able to recover. The problem, though, was that my confidence was beginning to erode. On the outside, everything looked great. On the inside, I felt like I was crumbling. But because I worked in the area of transformation, I kept putting pressure on myself to simply rethink my perspective. Easier said than done.

I felt too ashamed to share how I was really feeling with anyone. On one particular occasion, I felt myself freezing up. I turned to my colleague for support. "Bad luck," she said. "Just get over it." What other choice did I have? Pulling myself together and just getting on with it was my forte after all.

It didn't take long though before the cracks began to appear. I was exhausted. And holding it together was starting to take its toll. There were times where the world of consulting left me feeling like a prostitute being sold to the highest bidder.

CITY LIVING

While the cracks were starting to appear at work for me, the cracks in Alexander's relationship with his father were also beginning to show. Being a full-time, single parent wasn't easy, and I'm not sure Ajwad realised the extent of the responsibility he had taken on.

I took Alexander to breakfast at a local café in Melbourne, and he broke down. He had tears rolling down his face. I encouraged him to tell me what was going on. It was awkward, as we were out in public, but eventually he opened up as best he could.

"I can't tell you how bad things are because I know I can't come and live with you!"

My heart felt like it would crack in two. He understood that my life wasn't set up for him living with me full-time. Not long before this incident in the café, I had become bored with suburbia. So rather than face my boredom, I did what I did best and uprooted myself once more. I moved into a fabulous apartment in the middle of the city and shared it with a wonderful woman, with whom I lived very easily.

She didn't mind having Alexander over on the weekends and was really loving towards him. Very soon, I promised my son, our home in the country would be finished, and that was where we would eventually spend our weekends. I was blissfully unaware of the impact of moving so often. Not to mention disrupting the peace Alexander had felt when I lived so close to Ajwad. I was still so unskilled at enjoying an ordinary existence.

How clearly I can now see that moving so often (and always having a new project) allowed me not to have to deal with any kind of repressed or painful emotions I was feeling. How different things might have been if I had learnt to address these troubling feelings then. How much pain I found in the future that could have been avoided entirely. But the question remains, would I have listened?

WALKING AWAY

I had been in my job for almost two years. After a miserly, three-week break during Christmas and after a year of travel, travel, travel, I was fretting over preparing for a program I was to lead. I thought that if I prepared like crazy, everything would be okay. Instead of enjoying my holidays, I worked all the way through them. And though I didn't realise it, my anxiety levels were sky high.

I was still so out of touch with the depths of my fear. Instead of dealing with myself and how I was feeling, I focused on perfecting the program that would help others deal with the way they were managing their own lives. I didn't dare take the time to sit with how I really felt. I didn't trust my own innate ability, yet here I was trying to support others as they connected with theirs. As long as I stayed driven, I didn't have to look at the way I really felt. And drive through I did. But I wouldn't be able to hide the fear I kept repressing for long.

On the morning of the program, I broke out in hives all over my body. My fear and repressed emotions were now physically manifesting. My colleague, apart from finding my breakout amusing, was one of the first people to notice how unhappy I was and encouraged me to put my happiness before work.

I had to face the depth of the unhappiness I was allowing

myself to tolerate. I also needed to admit that I simply wasn't coping very well with life. Not with being a mother, and certainly not with doing my job. And though I always held it together in front of clients, I was falling apart inside. Exhaustion combined with compromised parenting left little room for happiness.

Absurdly, I would wonder to myself why I was so tired.

My resentment was mounting. I was resentful of so much travel. Resentful of my parenting arrangement. I was back to being the full-time parent. Alexander and I silently craved the old days, the days when I drove him to school, picked him up, had dinner ready on the table, and read stories before bedtime. The simple days coloured with ordinary comfort. The thing is, though, when I had that simple life, I didn't know how to be happy with it. Having a slow life while everyone else was so busy being 'successful' left me feeling lonely. It made me feel like I was missing out on something, or perhaps doing something wrong.

When I would express how I was feeling at work, I was told that it was how I related to the work and my life that was the issue. Not the work itself. While I knew all about mindset, how do you 'think' yourself out of sheer exhaustion? And what about my son?

Maybe they were right. Perhaps it was the way I was relating to work that was the issue; that I had come to believe it was more important than me. I feared I would never find another job that gave me the same meaning this job did. I felt aligned with so much of what the company stood for. But I just couldn't manage being a good mother as well as being good at my job. Something had to give.

There came a time soon after that pivotal conversation with my colleague that I found the courage to walk away. I had no other source of income and no idea how I would pay my bills. What I did know was that my life wasn't working, and I couldn't go on living the way I was.

Where I got the courage to leave a good-paying job whilst I had rent to pay, a mortgage to pay, and a child to support, I'll never know. But I trusted in one thing, which was what would ultimately see me through. I knew that when I lived with integrity towards myself, the universe would provide.

So I resigned.

This doesn't mean that after the courage to leave my job, the *Oh shit, what have I done?* didn't follow. Regardless though, I felt a huge amount of energy and freedom. One so familiar to me when I am fully in sync with who I really am.

True to my beliefs, the universe did indeed provide. Within three weeks, I got a regular consulting gig with one of Australia's largest companies. I began taking on my own coaching clients again. I doubled my income and worked half the time. And I didn't have to travel anywhere.

This lasted about a year. But I still wasn't feeling settled. It didn't matter how much value people told me I provided through my work. Something inside was always missing. I could see so clearly what others needed. Why couldn't I do the same for myself?

Once again, I did what I did best: I escaped. I took a three-month trip to Lebanon. I synchronised my trip with Ajwad and Alexander who also went to Lebanon. When I returned to Australia, I resumed consulting and was then offered a senior role in Sydney. Ajwad had been urging me to move to Sydney for years. He was completely supportive of this move with Alexander, who was also ready for change.

So just as I was settling into my newly built home in the country and enjoying my time in the city, I accepted the job in Sydney.

LONELINESS IN PARADISE

I moved up to Sydney before Alexander in order to set up a home that was ready for him to begin his new life and his new school. A private school. I was thrilled. For years I had prayed, *Please, God, help me to afford a private education for my son in his last two years of school.* Doing well at this point would better his chances of getting into the university course of his choice, and given that I'd messed up my own final year, I was desperate to see him thrive. And finally, this was possible. I'd done it. After years of budgeting my life away, I made a decision to live it up. So live it up we did.

The television I'd owned for fifteen years was replaced. I gave Alexander the car I'd had for sixteen years. I bought myself my first ever brand-new car. A convertible. I furnished the house to my heart's desire. No expense was spared. What else was I supposed to do with all the money I was making? Our first rental home had three living areas, four bedrooms, and two bathrooms. I filled them all.

Then came the world of working in an office full-time. After years of consulting and working from home in-between, this came as quite the adjustment. I didn't know what to do with myself. I bought a tea set so I could offer people tea when they dropped in. I tried to create this homey atmosphere at work, but then worried I was beginning to look like a crystal healing lady rather than a powerful member of the executive team.

I was the only woman on the team, which left me feeling incredibly lonely at times. I had no girlfriends, nothing to do, and no one to do it with in this new city. If a full-time job working nine-to-five in an office wasn't bad enough, suburbia nearly killed my soul.

Before Alexander arrived, I remember feeling an unbearable loneliness. I knew I needed to create a new social circle, but first I had to shake the desolation I felt. The first step was to stop feeling sorry for myself. Who was I to complain? I had it all…right?

I'll never forget the day I decided to get over myself and take a walk around the neighbourhood. I'd found the house online and moved in without ever taking a look around. My main criteria was to find a place close to Alexander's school, so he could be close to new friends. Apart from that, I looked no further. So what I found took my breath away. I was right next to a gorgeous forest track that wrapped around Sydney's middle harbour. Who knew the harbour was so close! Here I was, surrounded by this magnificent beauty, and only fifteen minutes away from the heart of the city. I was speechless.

Then I saw all the other houses nestled comfortably along the harbour shore. The architecture was stunning. It was hard to believe this was my neighbourhood. This was where I lived. I called Mum and told her I thought I might have just joined the ranks of the rich and famous. I felt like a peasant who had just been let out of the village. I (almost) couldn't believe this was my life.

LOSING IT!

Alexander was sixteen when he joined me in Sydney. He seemed to fit in quite well with his new school friends. They were truly the kindest teenagers we had ever met. They welcomed Alexander into the fold with open arms. Our home was constantly swamped with teenagers. I'd come home to find fifteen of them lounging about everywhere. I wanted them around, I loved it, but also desperately needed my quiet time after work.

After some time, the emptiness of the hype began to sink in. Alexander felt the need for a close friend he could really count on. While he had heaps of friends, there wasn't one he was truly close to. I think he, too, started to feel lonely. We were both so accustomed to having extended family around. We were also used to Melbourne and its more ordinary pace.

This new life of luxury was also taking its toll. Alexander became overwhelmed. The beautiful, big house, the swimming pool, a huge bedroom, great new friends who all had 'normal' upbringings. It brought up all the dysfunction of our life and made Alexander feel inferior to his new friends. They'd all grown up in the same house all their lives, with parents who were still together.

He tried to share his feelings. But I couldn't hear them. I

just felt unappreciated for all I was trying to create. But mostly, it broke my heart that my son wanted what I could never give him: Mummy and Daddy. A family home. He began to show signs of depression, and it terrified me. I had no idea how to deal with it. I was trying desperately to provide a good life, but I was lonely, and Alexander seemed depressed.

Perfect.

There was too much change for Alexander and I to digest all at once. We'd never spent this much time together, never been one hundred percent on our own. Ajwad had decided to leave Sydney, as it was not working out for him, and the seven days a week, twenty-four hours a day Alexander and I spent together was proving to be rather difficult to say the least. Before we moved to Sydney, I would go out on the weekends when I didn't have Alexander. I got a break. It was the perfect amount of together and apart. Now we fought all the time. I was at my wits' end.

We were having a major blowout almost every week. And in between these fights, I was exhausted. I knew I needed help. After all, I now had a teenager. And this, I quickly learnt, required a whole new set of skills.

Alexander wasn't afraid to tell me how he felt.

"You are really great, Mum," he told me. "Then you ruin it with one little thing. You just lose it, and I can't deal with it."

One night, after yet another blowout, I searched for a counsellor specialising in teenagers. I'm lucky in the fact that Alexander was very open to counselling. We found a woman he resonated with, and I found a counsellor of my own. As it turned out, this would be our saving grace. It wasn't perfect by any means, but I finally had support. Emotional support. And this was what I needed at that time. As well as some instruction on how to deal with raising a teenager.

I learnt so much in counselling! I found out how important separation was. Alexander and I were very close. And very dependent on each other. There was so much we needed to learn, and as uncomfortable as the separation between us was, we muddled through. Counselling was the best thing I could have done for us at that time. And we learnt so much about ourselves in the process.

This was also the year we had an exchange student come stay with us. Uri. He stayed for one term, and having him was wonderful. He and Alexander became like brothers. I got another son. We felt like a family.

Uri thought I was the most understanding mother in the world. Alexander thought I was unfair. He repeatedly told me how unreasonable I was. Uri was shocked at the way Alexander and I would blow up at each other, and then at how we discussed and resolved our issue. He'd not experienced anything like this before. Such freedom of expression, and hanging in there until we had resolution.

As frustrating as our relationship could be, Alexander was still my world. My reason for achieving. The reason I wanted to strive for a better life. But was *this* really a better life?

Was this what he really needed?

MOVING... AGAIN

Whilst living in the fabulous house with the pool I barely used and a house that took all day to clean, my landlords decided to raise my rent by three hundred dollars a week. Although I could afford it, it still felt like a slap in the face. Was I only working to pay the rent? So I planned a move to a house just around the corner.

The house I found had a stunning view of Sydney's middle harbour and a national park. It was like living in paradise, although the house itself wasn't in the best shape. I didn't mind, as I love a little grunge, but not Alexander. He loved our polished home that had a view of a brown brick wall. He vehemently opposed the move, refusing to lift a finger to help in any way. Seeing as I felt we were moving to heaven, I didn't argue. I just paid for help. I had the money, but not the energy to argue. The new house had a pool that overlooked the harbour. When I was home, I didn't want to leave. Who needed a holiday when they had this view?

Whilst speaking to Alexander's counsellor, she asked me to list all the moves Alexander and I had made, and the cities and towns we'd lived in. The list went something like this: Brunswick, Brunswick, Brunswick, Coburg, West Brunswick, Northcote, South Yarra, South Yarra, Williamstown, South

Yarra again, back to Brunswick, South Melbourne, Fawkner, Melbourne City, Brunswick, then we moved to Sydney and lived in Castlecrag, and then Castlecrag once more. I felt embarrassed when I put this list together. Never before did I have to confront how much I had moved my son around. No wonder he was shitty.

And there would be more to follow.

SELLING OUT

While there was a lot at home that wasn't working, my job was still going quite well. Within nine months of starting my new position, my boss got a promotion. He asked me to move with him and offered me a national role...which involved travel. Apparently, I had amnesia about my hate of travel and work, because I accepted this new role. I was afraid not to. What if I were to miss out on something?

Deep down, I knew I was selling out on my commitment not to travel. Just as I did with other feelings I didn't want to look at, I quickly pushed this thought down where I didn't have to deal with it.

My new travel schedule was going to be hectic, not to mention the fact that Alexander would soon be starting his final year of high school. So I asked my mother to come stay with me so Alexander would not be alone when I travelled.

Alexander started his final year of high school with gusto, taking on seven subjects, three of which were considered major projects. One was to turn a shipping container into a tiny house, one was a major art project, and then there was taking on three viva voce pieces for his music subject.

He was his mother's son!

I was unaware of Sydney's school system but later found

out that the recommendation was to take on only one major project during your Higher School Certificate (HSC). I had to beg him to drop down to five subjects. I went to war with him about it, actually. Go figure.

Despite dropping to five subjects, the load must have still been too much. He got sick and ended up taking almost two months off during his HSC. The problem, though, was that no one could figure out what was wrong with him. I quietly blamed myself and my going back to travelling. I couldn't help but wonder if my absence pained him despite our so-called lovely life. Eventually, I found an amazing holistic doctor who was able to get him back on his feet. This would be the beginning of many bouts of illness, though.

I also had myself checked out by the same doctor. I joked with her that I wasn't as bad as Alexander, but she told me that I was, in fact, much worse. I barely allowed myself to hear it. I didn't have time to be sick. But Alexander and I took our supplements, changed our diets, and I just got on with it. It wasn't like I could take a break in the midst of Alexander's HSC.

This isn't to say that there weren't good things that happened during this time. Because of my tumultuous relationship with Mum over the years, Alexander was not so close to her. However, during her time in Sydney, she became the awesome Lebanese grandmother. She made him his favourite foods. They argued adorably over Mum's commentary whilst watching movies. Alexander was the only person I knew that could shush Mum up without her getting offended. A love affair was emerging between the two, and I delighted in watching it unfold.

The cracks were beginning to deepen though. It started

with constant fatigue, yet I still couldn't understand what was wrong with me. I had a new job that I loved, a mum around to support me, and an abundant life, so why was I still struggling? I was convinced it was somehow my fault. That there must be something I wasn't doing right. Every weekend was spent on the couch, recovering from the week before. I had energy for nothing but the basics.

With me having nothing left in my tank to give at the end of the day or on the weekend, Mum became lonely. Depressed from being stuck all alone in beautiful suburbia. I reacted quite strongly to her emotional state. She tried to understand that I needed space at the end of my day, but still I could feel her need, and at other times, her understandable resentment. I simply couldn't deal with having another person who needed something from me. And as much as I needed her at this time, I decided it was best if I went at it alone. I couldn't take on one more thing.

When I mentioned to my boss that it might be wise for me to go down to four days a week, he asked why I couldn't just pay someone to help with my son. I felt so let down. Alone. Try as I did, I still couldn't seem to juggle work, parenting, and me. And I kept wondering what was wrong with me for not being stronger. Others seemed to be doing just fine.

Getting Alexander through HSC became my number one priority. Who cared if I couldn't see straight and was practically falling over from exhaustion? I had messed up my own HSC, my poor grades unable to get me into university, and paid a high price because of it. I would not let the same happen to my son. His counsellor was quick to point out that my anxieties from my past were getting in the way. Alexander was quick to point out that I acted as if it was 'all about me.' I simply didn't care. This was one time he could hate me as much as he wanted. I knew he would appreciate it in the years to come.

During HSC, we walked a fine line between having Alexander not overextend himself and him getting his work done. Once he recovered from being sick, his social life again became his passion. And while this did wonders for him as a person, all the partying began to take a toll on his body. The overextended social life he engaged during HSC resulted in a fatty liver and multiple throat infections that kept us in the hospital on a regular basis.

OVER-STIMULATED, OVER-SCHEDULED, AND EXHAUSTED

The year of Alexander's HSC, there was little relief. As the travel demands of my job steadily increased, my nervous system became overloaded. Once, as I was helping Alexander out of the house to get to hospital yet again, my boss called to point out that an email I had written was substandard. My boss, with his own stress in a new role, was let down by my work. But I was let down by my boss, who wasn't giving me the support I needed. After he suggested I hire someone to help with Alexander, I knew there was no way he would ever understand my world. I felt like a failure. Both as a mother and an employee.

I was starting to get treated like I wasn't part of the team at work. My boss would make cutting remarks in front of my co-workers. At one point, he even passed on my work to another team member right in front of me. Even though I knew certain pieces of the work were better placed with them, there was irritation in his tone and not a flicker of concern about my son. There was a deep shame around not being able to manage being both mother and a good employee. Like everyone but me had it together.

Towards the end of the year, I really needed a weekend to myself. Alexander had finished his HSC by then, so I planned a weekend at my home in Melbourne. He got sick almost the day I left. I asked the wife of one of my colleagues to check in on him whilst I was away. And when things did not get any better, I asked the doctor if she would swing by and look in on him. Bless her, she did this, but when she was there she called to let me know that Alexander needed to go to the hospital. Again. I lost it. All I needed was one bloody weekend to myself. No, it wasn't his fault, but I was beyond exhausted.

By the time I had paid for every holistic treatment available, the therapy, and every supplement on the planet, it began to feel like I was working for the rent and Alexander's well-being. Not to mention my own. Massages became a regular source of sanity. Having a working mum stressed Alexander, and working so much and being away from him stressed me, keeping us in a vicious cycle. This is when I really began to question what the point of it all was.

I reasoned that perhaps the growth required to survive this time of life was the point. This was the first time ever that I couldn't just pick up and leave. I could no longer use my favourite strategy: escape.

Then, out of nowhere, a wonderful DVD came my way: *Yogawoman*. It talked about the over-stimulated, over-scheduled, multi-tasking modern woman. It talked about me and spoke directly to me. I broke down and sobbed. It was the first time, in a long time, that my life made sense.

Before this, I had no words for why my life wasn't working.

Mostly, I would wonder what ever happened to strong Cindy. I felt so disconnected from who I was. The world I had created, the world I'd dreamt of for so long, wasn't providing what I needed. The joy, love, and fulfillment. Life was starting to feel hopeless. But if this wasn't it, what was? This was the thought that terrified me the most. So I just pushed on. But I did so with a newfound realisation: my exhaustion wasn't only valid, I was also not the only one who felt this way. There's a deep comfort in knowing your struggle isn't yours alone.

QUESTIONING MY PATH

I would be lying if I didn't say Alexander's last year of school nearly killed me. The last few weeks of HSC were absolutely wild. The grand finale after a year that had been hell. I don't think either of us will ever forget the night before his art project was due. I tried helping him, a mistake that led to him blowing up at me. Somehow, though, he made it through. And just as his teacher was beginning to think Alexander wouldn't be able to pull it off, he did. His teacher was ecstatic with the final result.

Then came time to finish the shipping container, the tiny home Alexander was building. Towards the end of the year, Alexander would get up early, grab my credit card, go get supplies from the hardware store, work on his tiny home, and then start his school day. I have no idea how he did it.

Ajwad flew up to help him during the last couple weeks. This tiny, sustainable home was fully insulated, equipped with working plumbing and electricity, a gas hot water system, and a fully-fitted shower and kitchen. It did, however, require a camping loo. And while there were fits and fights, the night he put his tiny home on display at school was a moment of deep pride and relief. We were all beaming.

His graduation was beautiful. I don't know how either of us survived the year, but we did. And the night was full of the most magical of feelings. I finally felt a semblance of achievement as a mother. I finally felt like I could exhale.

With HSC over, Alexander was jubilant. He said no matter how hard things had been, moving to Sydney had been the best decision I had ever made. The small blessings that are often found in disguise. I must admit, the stretching that Sydney required shaped me in ways that would have never happened if I had stayed in Melbourne. But what I learnt did come at a cost, and there have been many times I've questioned the path I chose. Sydney, however, had forced us to learn so much, especially about ourselves and our relationship.

From a young age, my son had a special quality. He was in tune with his emotions and the emotional state of others. When he was eight, he told me not to emotionally blackmail him. And on another occasion, when he was around ten, and I was stressed as we drove somewhere in the car, he gently put his hand on me and said, "Breathe, Mum."

One day, after a particularly upsetting event when he was around seventeen, he was lying on the couch. I asked if I could get him anything.

"No, Mum. I just need to be with my feelings."

In many ways, Alexander became my biggest teacher. He knew when I wasn't present. When we would go to war about this or that, and I would defend myself, he would calmly tell me, "I understand what I did wrong, Mum, but I can't be responsible for the extent of your reaction. That has nothing to do with me." When I would fall into my seduction mode to get him to do something, he was onto me. "Don't give me all that shit," he would say. "Just tell me what your request is."

With Alexander, there was simply no hiding. I both loved and hated it.

GOODBYE GARDENS, GOODBYE SWIMMING POOLS, AND BREAKFAST ON THE WEEKENDS

Alexander was now finished with school, and I was finished with suburbia. I began planning another move. I knew I had to get out of the stagnancy of suburbia lest I crack from loneliness.

Apart from the fact that perfectly beautiful suburbia had me feeling like a 1950s housewife, I was starting to isolate myself in this lovely paradise. And although Alexander revolted against my decision to move once again, I knew if I stayed, I was slowly going to lose my mind.

The move to Paddington showed some serious signs of struggle. I moved from my gorgeous two-story, three-bedroom, three-bathroom home with a pool to a tiny, yet lovely three-story cottage. This would be my first downsize. The lounge room couldn't even fit one part of my huge lounge suite.

Ajwad was the one who came to my rescue during this move. Like me, he didn't feel bothered by moving. If there was one thing we agreed on, it was our 'just get on with it' attitude. All the furniture I couldn't fit into my new place went into

Alexander's shipping container house, which we arranged to send to Melbourne.

With Ajwad in the picture and by Alexander's side, the move suddenly didn't seem to be so overwhelming for him. Or me. And somehow we managed to squeeze into this tiny, yet gorgeously homey, new house in Paddington. No more gardens and no more pools. Only one bathroom to clean. I was in heaven.

I felt completely at home in this little hub. On the weekends, I walked around the corner to my yoga class. Then, I'd mosey around the other corner for my tango lesson. Alexander and I had a breakfast ritual on the weekends. He walked to work and rode his bike to university. His friends came over, and they loved this new, inner city spot. I adored my life in Paddington and regretted not doing it sooner.

THROWING MONEY AT A PROBLEM

During these years, I found a new strategy for survival: throwing money at a problem. It was the easy way out. I shopped for convenience. I rationalised internally, *Thank God I even have money*. When I was too tired to cook, we went out to dinner. What teenager says to his mum that all he needs is home-cooked food?

Despite graduating with a great high school score and entering the world of being an adult, Alexander still needed me. Now more than ever it seemed. He loved my input on what to do with his life. He needed time with me to figure out all his options. He needed a strong parent to push up against to work himself out. The problem with my fast-paced lifestyle, though, was that it left very little in the parenting tank. What money will never buy is the quality of our presence and attention. In the absence of this presence, no matter how good the intention may be, all efforts will be unappreciated. And no amount of money will ever compensate for lack of parental presence. How it would break my heart when my son would tell me he just needed me to be present. I was constantly exhausted, which made my needing to be present yet another thing to do.

He was accustomed to the earlier years, when my pace was slower. When we had a simple routine. The days when we lived on my single parent pension and PhD scholarship. In hindsight, those years seemed far more wholesome. Alexander and I would reminisce on the simplicity and joy of those days. We referred to them as 'the good old days.' When I reflect on it all, I feel deep sadness and regret. I missed out. He missed out. I am aware, however, that many amazing things came out of this phase of our lives. One of which was how little I needed in order to be happy.

As I reflected on the source of the pattern that had become my current life, I began to see that it started with how my father showed he loved us. He was poor growing up and worked hard to make money; he truly believed giving us money was the same as giving us love and attention. I took on this behaviour, the undercurrent of scarcity that was passed onto me unconsciously.

I will never forget the time Alexander called home while he was travelling on his gap year. He called to ask if I would send him a package. Just a box with some vegemite, Tim Tams, and other little bits and pieces that reminded him of home.

"Can't I just transfer you some money, instead?" I asked.

"But all my friends are getting packages from their parents," Alexander told me, the disappointment apparent in his voice.

This broke my heart. I was finally able to see how little time and importance I put on the special things. Those gestures that no amount of money could make up for. Like the lovely feeling you get when you are travelling and receive a package from home. A reminder that you are not alone in the world. No one had ever done that for me, so how was I to know to do it for my son?

But when I tried to make up for it and told him of course I would send him a box, he refused to let me. It was too late.

SICK AND TIRED OF BEING SICK AND TIRED

Just as I was beginning to find home life to be more enjoyable, the mining and construction industry began to experience a serious downturn. The high-powered work environment where everyone felt like a superhero took on a completely different tone. The bottom line was suffering, and troubled projects became the norm. There were many restructures. Leaders pushed aside for failed results. Egos were crushed and the love disappeared. Work was suddenly feeling quite toxic and unsafe.

Alexander had gone off travelling for six months, which made it possible to travel more for work and not be home so much. It was a distraction from my now empty nest. I'd spend my days travelling from work project to work project, one day in the Pilbara, the next, four thousand kilometers away in Coffs Harbour. It was not unusual to spend only five nights a month in my own bed. A new level of exhaustion set in. A new pain that filled me with darkness and despair. Not only was I exhausted, I was on empty.

I went to my therapist, telling her I couldn't live like this anymore. I was at my wits' end. I asked her for drugs. Something to take away the pain. This new, agonising pain that loved to come and visit, especially on a weekend. She encouraged me to feel my feelings. No drugs. I began to question the point of therapy. Nothing seemed to work.

There were so many moments I just wanted to quit and go back home to Melbourne. But I couldn't do this. Alexander was very settled in his social circle and had truly wonderful friends. There was no way I could move him yet again, and at barely eighteen, I didn't feel he was ready to leave home and live in Sydney with no parent closeby. And as much as I wanted to once again just up and leave, it didn't feel right. Besides, I had also been encouraged not to keep running from my struggles. I was supposed to be feeling my feelings.

It didn't take long for my confidence to take a beating. My physical health was no better. Looking back, this is when my anxiety started to take a greater hold. But I knew little about the world of anxiety and would have never made such a link. I had joined the rat race after trying my entire life not to get trapped in it. But here I was, facing a lesson in endurance of the toughest kind. I was living on a diet of Panadol, tea, vitamins, and supplements. I had a constant lump in my throat. On the weekends, while the sky was a perfect blue, I could barely get out of bed. I was constantly sick, constantly tired, and embarrassed to have to constantly admit this. A deep shame began to take hold.

I was sick and tired of being sick and tired, but I couldn't see a clear way out. I began to wonder what I would do if I no longer followed my career path. There had to be another way. Something had to change, but what that something was, I had no idea. What really inspired me? I no longer knew. I had achieved all the things I set out to achieve, but what was it all for? I knew I needed to reflect on what really mattered to me, but anything I felt inspired about wouldn't pay the rent.

My work-life was a daily hit of one hundred emails. One day I reached the tragic realisation that the joy in my day amounted to pressing the delete button on yet another email. Sadly, this was what my life had been reduced to. I knew there had to be more to my life than to press delete.

In addition to my daily hit of emails, I was working on projects that were in crisis, where morale was low. These stressful environments were having an impact on me, though I was unaware of it. Supporting the projects made me feel useful, though, so I just kept going. As time went on, I began to fantasise about being a checkout chick that went to her job in the morning and then left at the end of the day, knowing her day's work was done. I didn't care about all the extra money anymore. I was too tired to enjoy it anyway. All I knew was that I wanted my old self back. I wanted to feel joy. So far it was all about accomplishment. But what was the point of accomplishment if I was too exhausted and empty to even enjoy it?

SYSTEM OVERLOAD

The entire time Alexander was away, I battled with insomnia. I simply couldn't sleep. The house was just too quiet. I was fighting the feelings that I didn't want to admit were surfacing. All the feelings I had pushed down over the years. My anxiety now shifted gears, and as if it wasn't bad enough to be passed out on my bed most weekends, I got to the point where listening and talking physically hurt.

At work, I could barely get through a coaching session without my chest wanting to explode. My head ached all over. My container was full. But listening and speaking was what I did for a living. This was terrifying. What was I supposed to do?

This pain was something I'd never felt before. I'd always delighted in supporting others. It was something that brought me joy, not distress. But I literally couldn't do it anymore.

I desperately needed to leave Sydney. I desperately needed to stop working. I was grateful for having focused on getting my mortgage paid off over the last few years. It was an obsession. Life was no longer about creating, it was about survival. About preparing for my exit from the workforce for a while.

Alexander used to ask me what the point of making so much money was if I couldn't enjoy it. By this point, I was too tired to enjoy anything. My nervous system could no longer deal with my lifestyle. It was in overload. I began to realise that people don't have nervous breakdowns. It's their nervous system that breaks down.

CONVERSATIONS WITH MY TANGO TEACHER

Who knew learning how to tango would be something that led to so much insight? One day, during a tango lesson, I suddenly pushed my teacher away with quite a jolt. I felt suffocated by the close embrace. "You know, there's only so much intimacy I can handle," I said.

This opened up a wonderful conversation between the two of us. One that allowed me to see the limit on my ability to truly be close to anyone. My relationship to learning tango changed that day. It was no longer about just the dance, it was about my relationship to myself, to other people, and to life itself. Tango was suddenly a wonderful metaphor for my life.

Here I was, yearning for intimacy but unable to sustain it even during something as simple as a dance. I learnt that I could not truly surrender to this dance or another until I first surrendered to myself. Surrender, not to be confused with submission, leaves no room to be in the past or the future; it demands being fully present in this moment.

And I was finally able to see, in real time, rather than just as a concept, how little I allowed myself the space to surrender to myself, let alone to another.

I learnt to relax whilst maintaining my own centre. This required self-confidence and individuality. Leaning in and leaning on, I discovered, were two different things entirely. It was all about opening up to the direction in which you were being led, whilst still holding your own. When led in tango, you become sensitive to the subtle cues, avoiding any kind of anticipation.

I found the rare moments in which I did relax into the tango dance to be ecstatic. But then I would pull back. My need for control was well entrenched. I would ask myself how much intimacy I could truly handle. Apparently, not much. Was I really willing to surrender? Not always. Surrender is a lovely idea, but who really does it willingly? But why, I would wonder, given the joy of surrender? Perhaps because just before real surrender, there is fear. Fear that must be faced.

DOWN ON MY KNEES

I began to feel there was nothing I could do to get relief from the senseless agony I felt. One day, when it all got to be too much, I simply got down on my knees and prayed to God. That's all that was left to do. I had exhausted all my other options. I wasn't exactly religious. Growing up in Lebanon had me equate religion with stupidity. War was raged in the name of religion. In the name of Allah. It never made any sense to me. I also had a grandmother who told us that if we didn't go to church, God would come down and choke us. It's easy to see why religion never resonated with me. I was desperate, however. I had nowhere else to go but down on my knees. But I found God didn't hear my prayers. Or perhaps it was just me. Maybe I didn't hear the messages.

It was so difficult for me to connect to any deeper part of myself at this time. I was lost. I felt desperate. I wanted God to take it all away. Make me instantly feel better. But I found it didn't work that way.

Still, I pushed on. What followed was a very rocky relationship with God. I'd reach out to Him, but then I'd break up with Him the minute things didn't go my way.

ACCOMPLISHMENT, ACCOMPLISHMENT...OH, ACCOMPLISHMENT!

I wondered for the hundredth time what the point of all this was. I had lived my life with the belief that anything was possible. I raised my son that way. I wanted him to know you could do anything you put your mind to. I truly believed in my dreams of grandeur. I was ambitious and believed in the power of commitment and doing whatever it took to fulfill my dreams. But I was starting to realise the high cost with which this came.

But I kept going. Striving for the elusive 'someday, one day when'... only to find out the view wasn't any better there.

I'd subscribed to the unconscious belief that with enough money all would be well, and that someday, one day when my house was paid off, or when I had enough money to relax and take a break, I would finally feel safe and secure. My pain and fears would be soothed.

So I went to work making sure financial security came first. I truly believed that financial success equalled safety, and I was also driven to prove I was not damaged goods. Eventually, I had an education, a career, and a house paid off. All of this accomplishment, and for what? I was exhausted and in emotional agony. Despite the pain, though, a yearning to go deeper continued to nag me. The need to let go of fear—the fear of everything falling apart.

I would ask myself, do I feel this way because of my current circumstances, or are these old and repressed feelings now resurfacing?

Was this the empty nest syndrome? Or was I just way off course?

After so many years of working on myself, I felt like I had my training wheels on all over again. Things stopped making sense. And as time moved on, they kept making less sense.

Perhaps it was time to disentangle myself from the fantasy I had made up about how my life was supposed to look and find out what really made me happy.

Along the way, I had confused my self-worth with what I had made of myself. I had lost touch with my real worth, which lay far beyond what I had made of myself. But I did not seem to be able to access it.

THE HARVARD GRADUATE AND THE FISHERMAN

There are times in our lives when we come across stories that shine the light on how crazy our modern day thinking has become. For me, this is one of them:

A vacationing American businessman standing on the pier of a quaint coastal fishing village in southern Mexico watched as a small boat with just one young Mexican fisherman pulled into the dock. Inside the small boat were several large yellowfin tuna. Enjoying the warmth of the early afternoon sun, the American complimented the Mexican on the quality of his fish.

"How long did it take you to catch them?" the American casually asked.

"Oh, a few hours," the fisherman replied.

"Why don't you stay out longer and catch more fish?" the American businessman then asked.

The Mexican warmly replied, "With this, I have more than enough to support my family's needs."

The businessman then became serious. "But what do you do with the rest of your time?"

Responding with a smile, the fisherman answered, "I sleep late, play with my children, watch ball games, and take siesta with my wife. Sometimes in the evenings, I take a stroll into the village to see my friends, play the guitar, sing a few songs..."

The American businessman impatiently interrupted. "Look, I have an MBA from Harvard, and I can help you to be more profitable. You can start by fishing several hours longer every day. You can then sell the extra fish you catch. With the extra money, you can buy a bigger boat. With the additional income that larger boat will bring, before long you can buy a second boat, then a third one, and so on, until you have an entire fleet of fishing boats."

Proud of his own sharp thinking, he excitedly elaborated a grand scheme which could bring even bigger profits. "Then, instead of selling your catch to a middleman, you'll be able to sell your fish directly to the processor, or even open your own cannery. Eventually, you could control the product, processing, and distribution. You could leave this tiny coastal village and move to Mexico City, or possibly even Los Angeles or New York City, where you could even further expand your enterprise."

Having never thought of such things, the fisherman asked, "But how long will all this take?"

After a rapid mental calculation, the Harvard MBA pronounced, "Probably about fifteen to twenty years, maybe less if you work really hard."

"And then what, señor?" asked the fisherman.

"Why, that's the best part!" answered the businessman with a laugh. "When the time is right, you would sell your company stock to the public and become very rich. You would make millions."

"Millions? Really? What would I do with it all?" asked the young fisherman in disbelief.

The businessman boasted, "Then you could happily retire with all the money you've made. You could move to a quaint coastal fishing village where you could sleep late, play with your grandchildren, watch ball games, and take siestas with your wife. You could stroll to the village in the evenings where you could play the guitar and sing with your friends all you want."

The fisherman frowned. "But señor...isn't that what I do now?"

So much for a Harvard MBA. It is the fisherman that teaches us what it means to really live. Given how little my life made sense, despite all that I had achieved, I knew I had to go back to basics and be willing to let go of all that I thought was important. That much I knew to be true.

KRYPTONITE

I am woman
I am successful
I feel empty

Illness strips away all excess, winnowing us down to the bare essentials. When the choice of denial has been stripped away, as it is in illness, we are brought face to face with our mortal selves, our tender vulnerabilities, the old wounds that linger in our hearts, the fragility of flesh, and the immensity of soul.
— Francis Weller

We must be willing to get rid of the life we planned, so as to have the life that is waiting.
— Joseph Campbell

BREAKING UP WITH LIFE AS I KNEW IT

While I wanted to take a break from working, there was simply too much to maintain. If I left Sydney, it would mean I would have to leave my son. On the other hand, to stay in Sydney required big overhead, which meant I had to work. In Sydney, even downsizing does not mean one cuts much in terms of expenses. I missed Melbourne. The thought of returning home felt safe. Manageable. I started to ache for the home I had built, but never truly lived in.

Alexander knew I was thinking about moving back to Melbourne and didn't like the idea at all. Why couldn't I just find a job with no travel in Sydney and stay? How could I explain to my son that I had no inspiration to find another corporate job? How was I to explain that I was scared? Scared to make the choice I knew I needed to make.

I asked myself questions that had me rooted in fear. If I left the corporate world, what would I do with the rest of my life? How would I make a living? Where had all my confidence gone? What was missing in all that I had been taught? Why couldn't I get in touch with my personal power? I longed to walk away and never look back, as if I needed to renounce the path I had travelled for so long. I needed to find the space to allow for a new path to emerge.

My confidence further eroded as did my health. During this time, I had an operation to remove some precancerous cells and barely gave myself time to recover. True to my superwoman style, I went back to work too soon. I simply felt bad taking too much time off. And with all the changes happening at the company I worked for, I felt I needed to make myself useful.

One day after returning to work too soon, I began to hemorrhage. So I calmly left work, got in my car, and drove to the hospital. I told only my boss. There I was, feeling completely alone as I was being pumped full of antibiotics to avert an infection. No one other than my boss knew to call to see how I was, yet I wondered why nobody cared. I was back at work a few days later.

Soon after, everything changed. My role was made redundant. A blessing in disguise. By then I had lost belief in the coaching profession. Who was I to coach others when I couldn't get my own act together? Something was missing, but I couldn't pinpoint what it was. My life simply wasn't working anymore. And I had ignored it for far too long.

I needed to find out what that missing piece really was. Given all that I knew and everything I had learnt, I was still facing the same old fears. Life might have looked better from the outside, but I still didn't feel whole. This better-looking life just felt like a cover up for the inadequacy I felt.

This was undoubtedly one of the scariest places I'd ever been. I could make my life look amazing, and sometimes I would even feel amazing, but it was all so fleeting. I knew I needed to look somewhere I never had before. I had to be brave enough to face that which I'd never had the courage to feel. So that's exactly what I did. And life had given me the push I needed.

I decided not to go back to work. It was time to get closer to nature. I decided to leave Sydney, leave my son, and go home, to Melbourne.

My role being made redundant made Alexander more understanding of my decision to move, and I was grateful that I had some money to support my transition. At least my next step was clear.

I would help Alexander find his own place, and then I would go *home*. I would take a year off to just have fun and figure out what to do with the rest of my life. A year seemed like plenty of time for such an inquiry.

How was I to know how much I would miscalculate this timeline?

As supportive as Alexander was, it was a transition that was also deeply emotional. He was happy to move out and live with his friends, but he still wanted Sundays in Sydney with Mum. Lunch once a week. Just the two of us. On one hand, it was exciting for him to move out. On the other, the pain of separation was often overwhelming. He loved family, and this was his first time living on his own. Once I felt Alexander was settled in his own flat, I would be able to move back home.

Making this last move was like walking through waist-high mud, though. I was exhausted beyond belief. The last few weeks I was still working in Sydney, I would come home and just crash. It made no sense. I was barely travelling and knew life was about to change. I was happy to be leaving, and work was a bit slower than what it usually was. And even though I had people to help me move, every little detail felt like a mountain that I had to climb.

Now, of course, I can see that it wasn't just the move. I was leaving my world as I had known it for twenty years. I had no clear future calling me forward. I was leaving my son who gave my life meaning. I was leaving the corporate world that gave me financial security. And although I was moving 'home', I had never lived in the country full-time. My high-octane superwoman wasn't just exhausted, she was on empty.

ADJUSTING TO COUNTRY LIVING

Regardless of how tired I was, and how hard everything felt, I knew I was making the right decision. Moving back home simply felt right. I couldn't wait to be in my own home.

I would study permaculture, master my yoga practice, walk the Camino de Santiago (a nine-hundred-kilometer pilgrimage across Spain), finish all the little projects that needed to be taken care of on the property, and figure out what to do with the rest of my life. I honestly felt like the luckiest person on the planet. All my hard work had finally paid off. I was so excited! I had been so responsible for so long, and now I could have my fun year.

I was able to finish the last month of my job from Melbourne, making me feel even luckier. The day my moving boxes arrived at the house, however, I simply collapsed in a heap. It was a workday, but I just couldn't keep my eyes open. Once again, it wasn't like I had to do much physically, which made me confused about my exhaustion. I couldn't figure out why I couldn't cope with things that used to come so easily.

Boxes decorated my house for days. I obviously hadn't known how easy I'd had it when trying to downsize in Sydney.

Here, it was almost impossible. I barely had any storage space, so I had to sort and choose what I wanted to keep. Just going through all my shampoos and jars of face cream was stressful. I had three of everything from the days when I'd had three bathrooms. I was so busy in Sydney that I'd just stocked up—the whole 'throwing money at a problem' thing.

The first few weeks back home, I had very little motivation to unpack. I used to be able to unpack and sort through things in one day. Not this time. I felt weak. Annoyed. I was frustrated with my lack of energy. It didn't make sense.

Why was I so damn tired?

I'd spent my life moving at fast-forward for years. What the hell was wrong with me now? Why couldn't I muster the energy to do something as simple as unpack and sort through my things?

There were other frustrations on top of the exhaustion, of course. And because I was so exhausted, they resulted in full-on emotional meltdowns. How was I to know that living in the country was going to be such a challenge!

The first major meltdown happened when the Internet technician informed me I could not get the Internet connected at my house. As much as I wanted to live in the country, I'd never considered that it would be without the Internet. I was outraged. Incensed. Couldn't think straight. All because of the damn Internet. Or lack thereof, I should say.

And although my neighbours were gracious enough to offer me their Internet anytime I wanted it, my inner-child was still sulking. I wanted my own stupid Internet connection. I had planned on completing certain online courses to help me with my transition. Not to mention all the movies I had planned to watch. The ones I'd never had time for. There wasn't a single café nearby that even had WiFi. Sure, I could have used the Internet at the library, but it was so slow it was more stressful to have the Internet than not.

I began to divide my time between my country home and Melbourne, which was a one hour and fifteen-minute drive away. I'd stay with friends and family and become a crazed woman, downloading all the things I needed for when I went home. I was obsessed. My detox from life in the fast lane was not comfortable in the slightest. I was simply addicted to my on-demand lifestyle. Whatever I wanted, exactly when I wanted it. And while my intellect knew how ridiculous I was being, my nervous system wasn't so understanding. That ugly part of me saying, "I want it, and I want it now!"

GAZING OUT THE WINDOW

It wasn't long before I was completely done with work and began to live my life fully in the country. When I arrived home, there on my table lay a book I'd purchased over ten years before. *A Course in Miracles.* In my thirties, the *Course*, as it was known, had been too confronting. I wasn't ready for what it had to say. This time, however, I knew things were different. I needed to complete the *Course*.

This would be my path to journey deeper within. My intellectual and material pursuits had both reached their limit. Now, it was time for my spiritual pursuit.

My days would disappear with me gazing out my window. I became fixated on the stunning view of the Mount Macedon Ranges and would find myself staring at their expansiveness for hours. I woke up to kangaroos outside my window, enthralled with breastfeeding joeys hopping in and out of their mother's pouch. I star-gazed at night. I meditated and did my lessons from the *Course*.

My life felt like a contradiction. Despite the feeling of emptiness, my life of speed and excess still had me so full I didn't need much stimulation. It was like I had to empty out the noise to fill up the emptiness. When people would ask me what I did all day, I would tell them my days were spent gazing out the window. But I quickly learnt that one of the biggest stresses I faced was not having a café just around the corner. As luck would have it, the local pub had closed down because of a kitchen fire. Overnight, I had to get used to cooking three meals a day. Just for me. This honestly started to feel like my full-time job. By the time breakfast was over and the dishes were done, it was time for lunch. By the time lunch was cleared away, it was time for dinner. I couldn't fathom how this had become my life. Existing simply to feed myself felt like a waste of my life. But who else was going to feed me?

I began to think this was what the rest of my life was going to be like. Living to make three meals a day and gaze out the window. Where would I ever find the time to make a living on top of all this cooking and cleaning when the time came?

Sometimes I would panic that I might get hungry at night and not have enough food in the house. No twenty-four hour anything in the country. What if I ran out of milk? What if I craved some chocolate at some unforsaken hour? As silly as they may now sound in hindsight, these were the thoughts that initially caused me some serious grief.

Slowly, this began to change. I eventually learnt where to go for good produce. I found an amazing grocer, open only on Thursday, Friday, and Saturday. All produce was sourced within one hundred kilometers, and the groceries were often harvested the same day they arrived at the store. The owners knew the farmers down to the quality of their soil. It felt so good to shop there. It became my favourite outing of the week.

Finding a routine around eating took months. Eventually, though, I found a cooking rhythm that didn't require me to cook every single day. And as I slowed down, I found blissful joy in these moments.

Until my head kicked in.

You need to be more productive. You need a project. Don't be lazy. What about everyone else who is working so hard?

They're just stupid, I would rationalise.

Who are you to think you can just laze about and do nothing but cook food and stare out the window? Life is stupid. How did you work so much for so long? You must be stupid.

Shut up! I would scream at these crazy making thoughts.

Another part of my transition to the country life was to go *au natural*. I would give myself haircuts on a whim. Use coconut oil as a hair treatment. Only use all-natural shampoo and conditioner. At one point, I was even attempting not to wash my hair at all. I read somewhere that this was good for your hair. I really did get a bit fundamentalist about it all. It didn't take me long, however, to find myself a hairdresser. I preferred peasant-chic to hobo-chic. I returned to the luxury products I was accustomed to, the ones that sold you on the idea that they were at least 95 percent natural. Yes, I still had a need to look good, even if I lived in the middle of nowhere.

Despite how well I started to adjust to country living, I began to feel I needed a bit more than sitting on my meditation couch and gazing out the window. I asked for guidance on which way to go. I suppose it came faintly, but mostly I didn't feel guided in any direction at all. I was still so full from my life on overdrive. There was one thing, though—I never questioned my decision to move home. I intuitively felt I was in the right place.

So I simply continued. My days passed by staring out the

window, making cups of tea, getting my groceries, feeding myself, connecting with friends over the phone, and...*poof!* The day was over. I would tell myself this would only last a few more weeks, and then I'd have the same get-up-and-go I always had.

But I underestimated the length of time this journey would take. I couldn't find the place where I could hear my inner-guidance speak. I used to be more connected to that part of myself. I wanted to get back to that place where I had my energy and all the answers needed to guide me to the new life I was desperately seeking. Nothing that used to make sense made sense anymore, though. It was like I was starting all over again.

GETTING IT ALL DONE

Now that I didn't have to accomplish anything regarding work and parenting, I turned my focus to all the things that needed attending to on the property. All the odds and ends I had never had time for during the last fifteen years.

Like everything in my life, I attacked these projects head on. Old habits die hard, and I was on a mission to get everything done. I could relax after everything was in order, I would tell myself. The sight of a dead tree would send me into a deep frenzy. I'd think I had to get it cut down and chopped up into firewood...*immediately*. My driveway had eroded, and I needed a new bridge for safe passage. Again, I could not relax until that was complete. Except it rained daily, which meant the project had to wait. I wanted to sort through my cupboards, sheds, and under the house so I could feel a little ordered. But with so little energy, those jobs took forever. With the belief that getting these things complete would free me up to really relax, my frustration soared with the snail pace of my new life. So much for wanting to slow down. I simply didn't know how to.

As soon as I closed out one project, however, five more would come to my attention. Getting closure had always been my go-to for reducing my overwhelm. For the most part, it was a successful strategy. I grew to rely on it. But this time, there was a problem. My body would simply not cooperate. Despite living a very low-key life, I was still so tired. All the time.

I would do thirty minutes of work in the garden and need to sleep for two hours. The mere thought of doing so little drove me crazy. Never mind the reality of doing so little. Moving through the to-do list I had created for myself, however, felt like I was yet again walking through waist-high mud.

I had always enjoyed the feeling of *doing*. But it wasn't working anymore. And being tired wasn't something I could just push through. When I did, it would only take me longer to recover. I knew deep down that the world wasn't going to end if I didn't make it through my list, but my inability to let go of getting it all done kept me frustrated and further exhausted.

I had slowed down my life on the outside, but for some reason, I just couldn't slow down the way I felt on the inside.

It was as if I was locked in some kind of automatic pattern that required me to go, go, go. And when I could no longer do this, I was truly at a loss for what I was supposed to do. Trying to slow down was much easier said than done.

On the occasions I would give myself the permission to go slow, I'd end up in a panic. One day, I decided I would spend the morning reading a book in bed. This lasted all of ten minutes (maybe), when out of nowhere, guilt jolted me out of my calm and restful space. Like I was supposed to be doing something. But I wasn't. As much as I wanted to stay in bed and simply read and enjoy this relaxed pace of life, the panic and guilt I felt wouldn't allow it.

Did I miss an email I had to respond to? Was there something important I had forgotten to do? Was I relaxing too much? Slacking off?

I noticed I would feel ashamed when people would ask me what I was doing, let alone when they asked what I was doing with my life. I could barely get through a small chore. How was I supposed to deal with the question of the rest of my life?

I began to preface the invitation to every social event with, *I'd love to, but I'm just warning you that on the day, I simply might not have the energy.* One day I had an appointment only thirty minutes away. When I returned home, I was done for the rest of the day. Exhausted.

I was talking to another woman who had left the corporate world. When she casually said that it had taken her two years to recover, I panicked. Would it really take me that long to get better? It was one of the most depressing thoughts I'd ever had. I had plans, so I had to get better. Very soon.

I became angry with myself for having pushed so hard for so many years. Blaming myself was the only thing I felt I could do. I told myself there wasn't any other reason for this fatigue. The thing I didn't have any compassion for, however, was how many major life-changing events I'd just experienced.

I'd moved, not only from Sydney to Melbourne, but from the city to ten acres in the middle of nowhere with kangaroos as my companions. I'd left my son in Sydney to be on his own for the first time, and I was no longer working. I also had no idea where I was going. The lack of compassion I had for myself left me in a state of frustration that was becoming all-too familiar.

There would be events that I really looked forward to attending, a simple permaculture event, for example. I would get extremely excited in the days leading up to it, then wake up on the day of the event, see the stunning blue sky, and know that it would be a wonderful time, but sadly feel too tired at the thought of being out all day. So I would cancel at the last minute. I slowly moved from blame to shame. I felt weak for feeling so weak. All I knew to do was push through, though. So I did.

I began doing yoga four or five times a week. The underlying belief in the yoga community is that even if you don't feel like it, you should still practice. Even when you felt sick or too tired. So I pushed through. Only in hindsight can I see the insanity. However, I was still in my automatic go, go, go mode. And the opinions of others were still able to easily sway me. Like there was a right way and a wrong way, rather than the way that worked for me in the moment.

HEALING TAKES TIME

When I first arrived in the country, I bumped into the husband of an old friend of mine. Later that night, my friend called me to welcome me to the area. She casually mentioned that her husband said that I looked haggard. I mean, it was true. I was exhausted, and I could barely move my neck from side to side. But that comment hit home.

I was haggard.

I knew I had to do something. I found a wonderful massage therapist who also saw how exhausted I truly was. I began to see her once a week. And as indulgent as I felt getting so many massages, I needed them terribly. The self-care I experienced in these early days of taking time off wasn't reserved strictly for massage. I found a chiropractor with whom a beautifully, synchronistic connection was formed. Not only did she help with the serious pain in my neck, but she also worked with my breath to loosen up my body. She taught me to observe without judgement. Observe without trying to fix what was wrong.

It was a slow process that sometimes felt like it was not working. But something kept me going back. Something deeply resonated with her approach to healing. It was like getting therapy through body and breath work. She always worked at my pace. Always gentle. Never pushing me to do more.

Through her respectful ways, I slowly began to change how I related to myself and my life. This was not, however, an easy unfolding.

AN ENCHANTED WONDERLAND

As exhausted as I was when first learning to enjoy this new chapter in my life, I did begin to discover accomplishment and wonder in the smallest of things. Such as the feeling of having my wheelbarrow in hand and walking down the hill to gather firewood. I marveled at how I could possibly own so much land.

The land captivated me. I started to form a dream about what the property would look like when all my projects were complete. I created a vision:

An enchanted wonderland overflowing with peace, love, and joy.

A place to be one with nature and one with self.

A paradise for my future grandchildren to inherit.

An area for my inner circle to share.

A place to rest a weary head.

Somewhere safe to reinvent life.

And rather than be driven by the need to complete tasks, I focused on this vision instead. And I gave myself the rest of my life to fulfill it. The aim was to enjoy its unfolding. But I was still in the early days of learning how to allow my life to unfold rather than how to make things happen. This subtle shift in relating to my life would eventually change everything. But there was much resistance yet to come.

JOY FOR NO REASON

After recovering from the shock of my move, and despite my exhaustion, I eventually fell into a sort of bliss. A deep joy so intense it shocked me. There wasn't any reason for it that I could identify. It just *was*. Joy for no particular reason, which was something I'd never experienced before. It felt like waves washing over me. Strong and powerful.

A Course in Miracles teaches that joy is our natural state, and all we have to do is remove the barriers to joy and love. When a person lives from love, when they learn the true meaning of forgiveness, and begin to trust in a higher guidance, joy is a natural result.

The *Course* suggests that joy is the indication that we're doing what we're supposed to be doing, that we are on the right path. For me, this was a huge insight. I had been chasing accomplishment my entire life. It had never occurred to me to follow my joy. Up until then, my life had been all about delayed gratification. Suffer now and be rewarded later. However, when life feels stressful or hard, these might be signs telling us we're not on the right path.

I have since learnt that despite my difficulties staying on this new path, there is a deep knowing that it's right. Not necessarily easy, but right. The *Course* tells us that the universe will gently guide us to where we need to be and will never tire of sending us messages. Just like a GPS never tires of redirecting us back to the correct route. The trouble is, we don't listen. Being driven to accomplish and learning to listen to this guidance are mutually exclusive. We're taught, it seems, not to listen to the gentle pull of what brings us joy. But there is a price for not listening. And I was paying it.

Over the last few years, I had fallen back into the trap of living from a place of fear and survival rather than trusting in the deeper knowing of my soul. Eventually, the universe stopped being so gentle with me. It screamed so loud that I had no choice but to begin to slow down and listen. But guidance would come in very strange ways, as if too simple to be considered guidance. Stop everything and relax. Let go of your to-do list for today, and go with the flow. On those days, strangely, I would accomplish more with less effort. There was a daily prayer in the *Course* that was recommended. We were told to ask God, the Universe, Life, the following questions each day or even each moment: *Where would You have me go? What would You have me do? What would You have me say, and to whom?* On the days I surrendered and trusted the answers to these questions, even the mundane began to offer deep joy. But this was not easy work. It took practice.

It eventually came to be that once I settled into my new country life, my purpose started to be about love, joy, and forgiveness. And while it sounds so good in theory, it is quite another thing to live from that place. And the things that brought me joy certainly didn't pay the bills.

I was also dealing with years of repressed emotions that

now had plenty of space to surface. For a while, they surfaced gently. After a while, however, I became flooded with emotions so painful I could barely contain them. I knew I needed to find balance in it all. I recall a quote, saying learning can happen quickly. It is unlearning that takes longer.

It felt like I had to unlearn everything I knew. Then I had to relearn. It was a constant work in progress. On many days, I was still able to feel my natural state of joy. It was no longer a concept I read about. I had attained it! But then I would try to hang onto it, and I quickly learnt that attachment is the antithesis to joy.

I would often forget that love, joy, and forgiveness were now my purpose. It was taking time to learn that I first had to love and forgive myself, and only then my actions would become clear. There were many layers of anger and rage I had to work through. Old feelings came on strong. Pushing, striving, and accomplishing had been my crutches for the past twenty years, and now I had no crutches at all.

I did a lot of sitting with these uncomfortable feelings. There was much to be untangled and felt. Despite knowing better, I still fell into the trap of blaming other people for making me feel a certain way. I began to realise the extent of the anger I held toward myself. Anger for all the times I had compromised myself in situations and relationships just to get the safety I desperately longed for. The whole forgiveness thing was proving to be quite the journey. Real forgiveness, I was learning, left me with a feeling of complete inner peace. But this peace was eluding me at times.

PERMACULTURE AND EX-CORPORATE CAPITALISM

If there was one thing that brought me joy, it was my permaculture courses. I loved them. Not only was it a great way to make new friends, but it was amazing to feel as if I was part of something. I loved knowing that I was gaining the knowledge that would allow me to manage the land in a responsible way.

My permaculture strategy was purposefully low maintenance. I knew I would never be the kind of person who could live in the country forever. Living off the land required a lot of work and demanded you be there every day. It was important, I learnt, to not only think in terms of environmental sustainability but to also think in terms of financial and energetic sustainability. Sharing my efforts with like-minded neighbours was recommended.

For a while, I shared chickens with the neighbours. I bought a couple chickens to add to their flock, and we would share in the buying of the food, as well as the eggs and manure the hens produced. Given my constant exhaustion, however, it was too much of an effort to even walk up the hill to get the eggs and contribute my fair share. My guilt set in no matter how understanding my neighbours were. Once again, though, I felt like a failure.

As amazing as my permaculture classes were, with all good things there is usually a downside. There are permaculture fanatics, many of whom are anti-capitalism. I don't blame them in the slightest, but there were times I felt like I was the ex-corporate capitalist. If I paid for someone to come do something for me, one of the permaculture participants would look down on me. Like, why wasn't I doing it myself?

I also felt a bit of shame around driving a convertible car. When I would give someone from my permaculture course a ride, the first thing they would do would be to comment on it. I can't tell you how many times I've heard "Nice car," and the many different tones it was said in—both genuine appreciation and contempt.

The feeling of anti-capitalism from some of the members of my permaculture society didn't surprise me. I simply come from a migrant family whose sole focus was accumulating wealth and investing. It's a mindset that was ingrained in me from a very young age.

For years, I was ashamed that I didn't have enough money. Ashamed that I didn't have all the sexy possessions I equated with having a good life. I declined dinner invitations because I couldn't afford it. And after working so hard to get where I was with a lovely house and car, I was suddenly ashamed of it. And while I know I had a choice not to feel this way, it didn't feel like it at the time. The feeling surprised me.

Despite there being judgement amongst the permaculture community, mostly there was a lot of kindness, wisdom, and those who walked the middle ground. I connected most with those people and was grateful for their friendship.

Whilst studying permaculture, I learnt about the importance of building social capital. This was a new concept that resonated deeply with me. The idea that there would one day come a point when people realised they could not eat money. When life became economically difficult, those who had the greatest social capital would suffer the least. The people would band together to offer the support one another needed. It reminded me of village life.

I began to focus on deepening the quality of my friendships. And while this wasn't easy due to my low energy levels, I knew in my heart it was important. I got closer to my family, my nieces and nephew. I cultivated local friendships. In this new country life, I began to experience a sense of belonging.

STACKING WOOD

Alexander finally visited me in the country. He loved our home, despite not making it down very often.

While he was busy on the phone, I meandered down to the front of the property. I had a little project there where I was trying to restore the property to its natural state. The big earthmoving machines that had dug trenches for phone and electricity lines many years before had left carnage in their wake. The front entrance to the property still looked like a construction site. There, I was pulling all the loose pieces of wood out of the piles of dirt, stacking them neatly to the side, and then raking the land back to its natural state. There was no real sense as to why I was doing this by hand to any onlooker. With a small machine, the job could have been done in twenty minutes. But I was delighting in it. Stacking wood was a meditation for me, and it gave me deep joy. So I followed it. I did say that the guidance I got did not always make any sense.

Then, when Alexander was done with all his social calls, he felt bored and even neglected, so he came down to join me. He almost had a fit. What the hell was I doing? Someone like me with so much potential, wasting my life away, stacking pieces of muddy wood into neat piles. He was clearly distressed. He thought I had truly lost my mind. Was this what I'd abandoned him for?

How did one begin to explain to their twenty-year-old son, who they had raised to believe they could do anything they put their mind to, that this was what I was putting my mind to? I thought it best to simply leave this job for the moment and go make a cup of tea for my son. I was barely able to understand my own actions, let alone explain them to him.

It was an adjustment for us all.

LOOKING MESSY

As I began to realise that my joy wouldn't come from 'getting somewhere,' I started to understand that in order to find joy, I must let go of my protective layers. These layers of striving, doing, and getting that I had accumulated and allowed to block the flow of joy that was my natural state.

I began to wonder what I could let go of that would allow my innate joy to flourish. I knew that the driven side of me wasn't going to go away overnight just because I now knew it was getting in the way. I was beginning to see I could even be driven about walking the middle road. So much learning. So much to undo.

All my crutches had to be dropped before I could experience real clarity and peace of mind. Surrender? Yeah, right! Non-judgement? Sure. Slowing down? Torture. Unconditional love? Only if there is something in it for me. Giving up my story? I didn't know who I was without it.

As much as I believed in these concepts, it was difficult for me to understand that they weren't somewhere to 'get to.' And all the while, I wondered how to truly bring them into practice in my day-to-day life. Practice them while paying the bills and and allowing myself to enjoy an ordinary existence. I knew that the material world didn't need to be ignored in service of the spiritual world, but I still had to learn to balance both.

For those of us who aren't going to be a Buddha, Jesus, Krishna, or Mohammed in this lifetime, how do we walk the middle road? How do we welcome life just the way it is? Welcome life from the essence of who we are rather than who we think we should be? I had to dare to trust my inner knowing versus my survival knowing. And I had to give this journey time. More time than I had initially planned.

At first, trusting my inner knowing was terrifying. I doubted my voice. My fear was still louder than my innate knowing. I hadn't yet learnt to trust it. Using my head wasn't going to work, no matter how many times I insisted on trying. I had to take small steps. I had to dare to stay in the void of not knowing what path I was supposed to choose. I had to find the courage to look messy to the people who saw me as strong, clear, and capable. It was a lesson in humility.

HURRY UP AND SLOW DOWN

As much as I tried to slow down and find a new way, my old way of living seemed to still be my current way. I was still being driven by an outcome. This time the outcome was slowing down. A noble pursuit, I must say. But all I felt was impatience. I had slowed down my physical life. Now the challenge was to slow down my mind.

I was addicted to thinking and analysing. Searching. Desperate to find a new passion. Something that would absorb me, the way my work once did. I was desperate for answers, but time felt like it was running out. My one year off was almost over, and all my over-analysing had done was get in the way of my simply enjoying each moment and allowing my life to unfold in its own way.

I believed I should have found the answers by now, and that I should have been feeling invigorated and back in touch with my real passion, whatever that was. However, this simply wasn't the case. Apparently, I had to go deeper. I was fast learning that exhaustion and inspiration were mutually exclusive. I simply needed more rest.

FREE FALLING

My brother was in Lebanon holidaying with his family when out of nowhere, a WhatsApp group was set up so he could share some news with me and my sisters: Dad was in hospital. My brother promised to keep us updated.

Then, of course, came the mind chatter. My thoughts that Dad was seriously ill and possibly dying drove me into a frenzy. And not a loving one. I was so angry! I had a few weeks left before I went on my three month trip to Europe. Three months of travel all for myself. Finally. I had waited twenty years for this trip that included my personal pilgrimage, the Camino de Santiago, a walk from France to Spain. And now it might get interrupted? Was I ever going to get a break?

How ugly these thoughts were! I was ashamed of having them. But these feelings and thoughts flooded in involuntarily.

It wasn't as if our family was run on obligation. Any feelings I had about needing to change my plans were ones I placed upon myself. At this point, I wasn't yet able to simply sit with my feelings. I resisted them instead and did what I'd always done best: judged them.

Then news came that there was nothing to worry about. Dad was going to be fine. Fluids had been pumped into him. The doctors put it all down to dehydration. Something still felt ominous, though. None of what we were told made much sense. My trip, however, was saved. I could finally get back to allowing life to unfold the way I wanted it to, or rather, how I hoped it would.

One day, soon after receiving news about Dad, I woke up with the sensation of free falling. The sensation of falling off a building with nothing to catch you. Even the safety of my mattress wasn't making me feel secure. I was terrified. I had no idea what was happening. I had no idea how this could be. *Again*. If it wasn't one thing, it was another. And so began my analysis once more.

Was this happening because I had too much space with all my projects temporarily completed? Did it have something to do with my studying the *Course*? Was it hidden fear from my past returning to haunt me?

Those three weeks before I was due to leave to walk the Camino, I couldn't shake the feeling of sheer, unrelenting terror. It was a constant feeling of being punched in the gut. I began to believe it would be like this for the rest of my life. Nothing could make me feel safe. I had felt bad before, but this was a whole new level. And try as I did, I couldn't figure out why.

I wondered if it had something to do with Dad's ill health. Was I tuning in to something being really wrong? Hadn't they just said it was dehydration and a stomach thing? All I knew was something felt very wrong. I wondered if I could even go travelling if this was what I was going to feel like. But it was times like this that my strategy of pushing through came in handy. I would go. I would take this pilgrimage.

Adventure beckoned. And when I finally boarded my plane, thankfully, the fear abated.

ALLOWING THE PATH TO UNFOLD

Most people who plan to walk the Camino de Santiago train for months. Up until the day I left, however, I still barely had the energy to get through the basics of my day, let alone train to walk a nine-hundred-kilometer pilgrimage with all possessions on my back.

But as Dad often reminded me, I was stubborn. And of this, I was proud. I decided I would go and just get fit along the way. Before leaving, I did manage a one-day course on how to prepare for the Camino. I was armed with a list of what I needed to take with me. I had my maps and backpack. All I needed was the equipment and clothing. How hard it had been to find the motivation to buy everything I needed, though! I was still ignoring the signs. I wasn't listening to what my body was trying to tell me. I had made up my mind, and I was going.

I can now see that I made this decision with my head rather than my heart. This meant I had to push rather than allow. I wasn't letting the path of my life naturally unfold. It was fine if it did so in a timeframe that was comfortable to me. If not, flow would need to kindly step to the side and allow for superwoman to take over. I still had to work out what to do with the rest of my life, mind you. And I only had three months left. Surely, this would be long enough—though it didn't feel that way when I began my journey. And rather than relax and just be, I found myself planning the after-trip in my head. I began to fantasise about always being on the road, so I wouldn't have to face the monotony of day-to-day life. As much as I told myself to just be, it was as if I were everywhere but where I actually was. A very familiar feeling.

On the Camino, my head was spinning with endless thoughts that kept me far from what was happening around me in the present moment. Thinking about everything about the journey rather than being one with the journey. Food for tomorrow. Confirm the hostel booking. Would I meet interesting people along the way? Would I be enlightened by the end of my pilgrimage? Would I have clear purpose and renewed direction? Would I find inspiration for the things I had already planned? This endless chatter in my mind was deafening.

I was surprised at how antisocial I initially felt when I first embarked on my journey to Santiago. When the pilgrimage began, the people around me simply annoyed me. I wanted solace. *Hi. What's your name? Where do you come from?* These simple questions got under my skin, especially when I felt no pull to talk to anyone. I wondered why this was, given how much I'd always loved to socialise.

I met a fabulous Spanish woman over dinner on the first night. She was full of life, and I was reminded how not full of life I really was. I also realised something else. When I felt irritated with others, I simply needed space. Time to be alone and be quiet. The Camino, however, wasn't exactly the best place to do this. Ever so gently, though, I started to open up to other people.

There were many learnings on the path. At times, I noticed how I would attach myself to someone in order to feel safe. Other times, I would get all worked up about having enough food or water to last my daily walk. Or that I would be left to sleep out in the cold even though I had reserved a bed in advance.

The Camino teaches you to trust that all will be well if you just surrender. I met a woman who taught me to just trust that the little food we had would be enough for our walk that day. Not long after, a man rode past and said he would not be eating his orange. He gave it to us, and we had a lovely morning tea sharing this one orange.

During this pilgrimage, I was reminded of how easily I got off centre. Even though I felt the need for solitude, I still wanted to join the fun people. To be full of life, like the Spanish woman I had met on the first night. I wanted to embrace the attention I got from men that really did nothing but distract me from my inner journey. I wondered why I couldn't be clear about my need for silence. I wondered why I couldn't simply stay present. And with each day that passed, I kept wondering what I would do with the rest of my life.

RETURNING HOME

For my entire pilgrimage, I didn't suffer from fatigue. But it returned the minute I stopped. I hadn't factored in the time it would take to recover from a nine-hundred-kilometer walk. I would get annoyed seeing my Camino friends post pictures online, still climbing mountains and travelling after they'd just done the same walk I had. Probably not the smartest thing to compare myself to twenty- and thirty-year-olds when I was forty-four. But my inner twenty- and thirty-year-old wanted to keep climbing mountains. I didn't want to miss out, but I didn't have a choice.

Low grade fatigue returned. And I knew I needed to rest. Despite the fact that the three months had come to an end, and I was exhausted, I had a deep urge to continue travelling. I loved life when it was lived on the road, and the urge to get back on it was strong. I loved the daily routine. Get up, get dressed, eat, and set out on the path despite not knowing where it would take me. Meet new people, arrive at the next destination, find a place to sleep, unpack, shower, eat, sleep. Simple.

Every day brought something new whilst at the same time living ever so simply. I loved my backpack and felt lost without it when I returned. My clothes, carefully chosen so I appreciated each separate item. I loved not having to decide what to wear each day. Just one or two options depending on the weather.

I believe the Camino shows each person something different. My Camino showed me that control was where my work was. Letting go of having to have everything mapped out to make me feel safe and secure. Surrendering to the unknown. Holding on to control left me feeling dead anyway, so why did I insist on holding on so tight?

My one year off had come and gone. I was supposed to have it all figured out by now, wasn't I? I knew I was still grasping at what little control I believed I had. I was just too scared to truly let go. And I still had no idea what letting go really looked like.

But hadn't I experienced deep joy during my year off? Where had it gone?

DEATH

I am woman
I don't know
I am terrified

You are so brave and quiet, I forget you are suffering.
— Ernest Hemingway

Everything we avoided for the sake of living in safety yields to a desire to encounter it all.
— Francis Weller

WHY CAN'T I GET MY ACT TOGETHER?

I was still driven by whether or not I was accomplishing enough in my life. So I began to reflect on what those accomplishments were, especially since taking a year off.

Well, I felt softer. I had lovely neighbours and friends in the country and felt like I belonged to a like-minded community. The country finally felt like home. I'd completed two permaculture courses, walked the Camino de Santiago, and completed many of my jobs on the property, albeit nowhere near everything I wanted to do. I had completed the three hundred and sixty-five lessons in the *Course* but unfortunately, did not feel the peace I had hoped for. And thankfully, after two years of tests, I no longer had any evidence of precancerous cells.

I had accomplished a lot, but it still didn't feel like *enough*, and something felt *wrong*. Inner peace was still intricately tied to the need to know what I wanted to do with my life.

I was back to suffering from low grade fatigue most days, as if some kind of poison was coursing through my veins. I could not figure out what the hell was wrong with me, nor could the doctors. I had really believed that I could sort out the rest of my life in one year, but life was simply not turning out the way I had planned. Not only was my health weak, I still had no clarity around *where to from here.*

That thought alone terrified me.

Other thoughts started to plague me, like, *What will people think of me if I am not really successful?* Feelings of jealousy when I would see other people move into more senior roles while I couldn't get inspired about, well, anything really. I was so emotionally and mentally exhausted and felt no excitement for any plan that came to mind. Everything that I was good at simply felt like more of the same thing that had brought me to this place to begin with. I had lost my fire. I was doubting that I would ever find it again. That feeling of excitement I used to have about life felt so far away from me, and it only added to my fear. Would I ever get my energy back? I began to fear losing everything I had worked so hard for. How would I pay the bills if I did not 'get my act together'? I kept asking myself why others were coping, and I was not. Would I become like Sylvia Plath, who once wrote what horrified her the most was the idea of being useless. Of being well-educated and brilliantly promising, and yet 'fading out into an indifferent middle age.' She was only thirty years old when she took her own life.

I would implode on myself with all those thoughts.

But I'd had a taste of deep joy. I knew what was possible. Those moments gave me faith that I was on the right path. But at times I damned that stupid path.

One day I would be having the most blissful day, lunching leisurely with a friend, admiring the trees in the botanical gardens, discussing future work plans. The next day, I could barely breathe from the terror that was ripping through my body.

On the days I would get respite from the fear, I focused my attention on returning to work. But still, I had no energy or inspiration for it. The thing that did inspire me about having a job was the promise of structure. A great team of people to interact with. Well, those things and the money.

Through my spiritual pursuits, I was learning that peace was not about having all my needs met. Love and peace abided deep inside me, and my job was to remove the barriers to reach them. The challenge was being able to remain at my centre, at my inner peace, whilst not having my needs met and not having everything around me as I would like it to be. Of this, I would remind myself daily. But peace would elude me no matter how hard I tried to be spiritual!

SEARCHING...SEARCHING... FOR THAT MISSING PIECE

I had learnt so much over the years on my quest for personal development and growth, yet the day had come when all that I had learnt no longer supported me. There was still a piece missing. But I could not figure out what it was. The harder I tried to figure it out, the less clarity I would get.

I knew I had to be patient and allow the answers to percolate to the surface, to allow them to come from deep inside. But I could not switch off my head. Having my life come to such a 'full stop' was hard, but I had no choice given my lack of energy. I kept waiting for clarity on what my next job should be or which new direction I should take in life.

My head would come up with lots of solutions, but none of them propelled me into action the way I used to be propelled before. And given that I did not have enough energy to push through my good ideas, I was forced to be patient. At times it was freeing, and at other times it drove me crazy.

Despite my attempts at patience, I still could not shift my need to keep planning, searching, questioning. It was exhausting. I could now see how much pressure I had put on myself to keep striving. But without my old driven ways, I found it hard to navigate.

Thankfully, there were still days where I would surrender to the delight of spending the day cooking, reading, and getting my life in simple order. These days filled me with peace and joy. I felt so complete in the ordinariness of it all. Other days, there just seemed to be so much in the way. Once upon a time, my deepest fear was to live a boring and ordinary existence. Now the ordinary filled my day and nourished my soul, when I allowed it to.

What was happening to the need to have my life amount to more? It would come, then go, only to come back again with greater force.

In this calm ordinary space, feelings of long repressed pain and anger began to surface. I would seethe about events that I thought I'd found forgiveness around. A hurtful comment a friend had made ten years ago. Events from childhood. Anger towards myself for putting up with things in silence. I wondered if this was good use of my time. But in the silence, in the space, up they came. Each one demanding new attention. Was this the reward for slowing down?

But still I followed my teachings. I learnt to allow my feelings of anger and pain to arise whilst also choosing forgiveness. It became my delicate work to do. Often the feelings were dense and didn't move quickly. And just for a little extra reward, my fear around finances began to surface. Fear that my life would fall apart if I didn't hurry up and get it together. On some days, I was able to just observe the fear and not react to it, but on other days, it would take its hold.

For years, I had learnt that my feelings were caused by how

I interpreted a situation. It was all a matter of perspective after all. So when strong feelings would arise, I would go to work on shifting my perspective. I had also learnt, though, that not all feelings belonged to the present moment. Some belonged to a time long passed, and some did not belong to me at all but had, perhaps, been inherited through my lineage. My lineage of massacres and starvation. So all the shifting of perspective was not going to shift my feelings; especially the ones that had been minimised or ignored for so long.

I had yet to learn the art of vulnerability—how to feel my feelings without blaming anyone or anything for them. But when the pain was too much, my way was still to attack and blame. *I deserved an apology*, or *Such and such a person needed to see the error of their ways*. Or *Why didn't I tell them to f' off? I shouldn't put up with people's shit*. The noise, once again, was deafening. I would cycle through seething, allowing, finding compassion, and taking responsibility, sprinkled with a healthy dose of resisting it all. Allowing the feelings to just be was not an easy road. But deep down, I knew this road of feeling your feelings was one I had to learn to walk. Repression and denial were just not working anymore. Over the years, I had developed a very skillful ability to shut my feelings down and just get on with it. I was a good, hard-working woman, and I was not going to be stopped by any circumstance, let alone feelings.

While inspiration for the rest of my life was slow to come, I continued to focus on all those things that still needed fixing in the house. At least it gave me focus. I learnt to build my own shelves from recycled materials. I learnt to use my electric drill that I had owned for seven years. I conquered those tiny tasks that had the ability to overwhelm me, like hanging up my clothes hooks, fixing my squeaky bed, re-attaching loose objects. Given that I had less money now, I had to be more creative and resourceful and to also ask for help. No more throwing money at a problem. It felt good.

But despite the joy I felt from the ordinary, I would still oscillate between loving it and needing to get away from it.

NOTHING TO HOLD ONTO AND NOWHERE TO GO

I was initially so relieved to take a break from parenting that I missed the signs of my grieving. When Alexander came into my life twenty years before, he filled it with purpose. What was the point of it all now? I had no idea what it would take to re-create my purpose beyond motherhood. Yes, there were difficult years. Yes, I needed a break. Yes, I wanted it to be easier at times. But never did I wish for it to be over.

With the empty nest came this slow kind of death. The death of motherhood as I knew it.

On the other hand, my leaving Alexander and returning home signified pure abandonment to him. So to add insult to injury, Alexander launched a full blown offensive against me. My leaving him in his younger years had come back to haunt me. Except this time he was not using being a 'good boy' as a means of getting Mum's love. Instead, his offensive included pointing out every last failing I had as a mother. Many of which I found hard to even defend. In my last year of being in Sydney, I had little resources left to keep myself in check as a mother. My stress often spilled over, damaging my relationship with Alexander and eroding his sense of safety at home.

So no matter how I tried to busy myself, I simply had too much space now. Where I once needed space to empty out the noise, I now needed more stimulation and something to do. The serenity was driving me crazy. And before long, a deep loneliness set in.

The free falling fear was back.

With no job to go to each day, I felt lost. With no son to take care of, I had no purpose. It was like being out at sea with no life raft and no land in sight. I had nothing to hold on to and nowhere to go. The void terrified me.

And then, on top of that, came more news: Dad had lung cancer.

*

Dad had returned from Lebanon to Australia just before Christmas to get some tests done. His regular check-up to make sure his emphysema and his stomach ulcer were in check. I had returned home from the Camino a few weeks after him. Whilst on holidays with my brother and my older sister and their families in Queensland, Dad had a seizure. He was out at dinner with them when it occurred. This elevated the urgency of Dad's health, but still the hospital did not uncover the extent of his health problems. They just thought he needed more oxygen, and that the lack of it caused his seizures. He was lucky not to be alone when this happened, and even luckier that he was not on an airplane.

A few months later, the results returned from the lung specialist which revealed the lung cancer. Getting a cancer diagnosis was one thing. Getting a stage IV lung cancer diagnosis was another thing altogether. Dad was now gripped by his own fear. So much so that he could not relay any clear information his doctor gave him back to us. It took a while for me to be sensitive to Dad's overwhelm. I was initially frustrated by his inability to interact with his doctor. He couldn't even place a simple phone call to make an appointment with a specialist. He kept asking for help with what seemed to be easy things.

Eventually, I realised Dad could not cope with his diagnosis as well as figure out how to navigate his way through. So I stepped in to at least get clear on some facts. I spoke to Dad's lung specialist. The verdict: Dad had six months to live.

We would be lucky to have him with us until Christmas.

Mum and Dad had been watching me while I was speaking to the doctor on the phone. I had an out of body experience while telling Dad what the doctor had said. I think Dad had a similar experience. It was surreal. Like a scene out of a movie. I felt numb. My own overwhelm and frustration immediately subsided. Compassion began to seep through me. My heart was breaking as I saw the terror in my father's face. How did one reconcile being told they were going to die in six months?

NAMING MY ANXIETY

It was becoming a common occurrence for me to wake up most days with fear and a constant buzz running beneath my skin. A subtle tremor of terror that never quite left me. It was time to admit that I might have anxiety.

So I bought my first book on anxiety, *My Age of Anxiety* by Scott Stossel. This book served to normalise my experience of anxiety. It may sound like a small thing, but buying this book was an important step for me. It was reassuring to know that I was in good company when it came to anxiety—George Cheyne, Charles Darwin, Sigmund Freud, William James, Carl Jung all suffered from anxiety. This fact diminished my shame. I concluded that perhaps anxiety was a path to deeper transformation. That was a soothing thought. I was not going mad after all. *Perhaps this is just normal?!* And so the self talk would go. Trying to convince myself that I was not going crazy. Sadly though, the author never recovered from his battle with anxiety, so I'm not sure it helped in terms of giving me hope.

I continued to use positive self talk: *I am strong. I will be loving and patient with myself. There is nothing wrong with me. I just don't feel great. Okay, I feel like shit. I feel proud of myself for admitting it is too much to deal with. I am tired of being tired. I'm tired of being ashamed of my anxiety and loneliness. It may be normal, it may be from childhood, it may be an existential crisis.*

I didn't care what it was, I just wanted it to end.

HOW THE HELL COULD THIS HAPPEN TO ME?

There was so much going on inside me. The fear now constant. A visit to my chiropractor provided some respite. She adjusted my neck, which gave me instant relief. She said the fight-or-flight part of my skull was getting activated by my neck being out of alignment. It was shocking to me to realise what the body can activate in us.

I was so focused on my inner world that I had lost sight of the power of managing my physical world.

But then, as if out of nowhere, the terror would return. Then came the added layer of fear. The fear that I would never stop feeling the terror that had an almost constant grip on me now. Shallow sleep made me appreciate any night where I was able to sink into deep rest. I would listen to anything that would soothe me—Eckhart Tolle's audio book, Adyashanti, *A Course in Miracles*. It would work, though only temporarily.

Now, rather than being fixated on searching for answers on what to do with the rest of my life, I became fixated on searching for answers on *how the hell this could happen to me*. I, who had so many tools, who had done years of therapy, who had worked so hard to live a powerful life. I was supposed to be a strong person. In all practicality, what on earth did I have to be so afraid of? The more I sank into hell, the crazier I felt. I felt weak and ashamed of feeling weak. So I began to isolate.

*

Dad had chosen to deal with his cancer the natural way. We had heard horror stories of the devastating impact chemotherapy could have on one's immune system, causing more damage than good. One uncle in particular was so depleted he could not stand the pain of someone lifting him as he was being taken to hospital. The information on treating and beating cancer was overwhelming and often contradictory. Many natural treatments promised to keep you alive but almost guaranteed to leave you broke given how much they cost. Eventually though, Dad began a simple routine of breathing exercises, gentle physical exercises in the park, natural therapies, Chinese herbs, and dietary changes to manage his cancer. Dad believed he could be cured and stayed positive.

One day, Dad began to experience pain in his shin. We dismissed it as a possible strain from his new exercise regime. Still inexperienced in the world of cancer, we were slow to realise the extent of Dad's situation, causing him to suffer far too long. Eventually he had his shin x-rayed, which revealed that Dad's cancer had spread and metastasised to the bone. That handled any denial that was at play. Dad was admitted to hospital immediately for radiotherapy. More scans would be administered to check for the extent of the spread.

With Dad being admitted to hospital, things got real. I slept in his bed at my parents' home that night and found a picture of a Lebanese saint under his pillow. For some reason, it broke my heart. I wondered about how scared Dad might be. He had never been religious. But I knew that feeling of desperation that drives us to reach to the saints and gods to get us through our terror.

Then it was confirmed: the cancer had spread to the brain.

A stillness fell over our entire family. Phone calls where not much was said, or *could* be said. Our family, despite our issues, always bonded in a crisis. New warmth and love emerged. Our conversations softened with each other. The reality of how delicate life was set in.

DARING TO DO NOTHING

Right around the time of learning that Dad's cancer had spread, a friend had recommended I read Joseph Jaworski's book, *Synchronicity: The Inner Path of Leadership*. 'But we are terrified that if we stop, we'll drown,' says Jaworski. This one sentence spoke to my inner world with such clarity. Coming across Jaworski's book taught me that sometimes the greatest act of commitment involves *doing nothing*. Up until now, I had felt guilty about doing nothing. Indulgent. This brought a new perspective on patiently waiting for the next step to reveal itself. To wait patiently for what was calling. 'When nothing is calling' he says, 'do nothing.' So rather than resist this new way as I had been doing, I began to embrace it.

I had emptied out a lot of noise from my life and had the space to truly stop. Still, it was terrifying. Doing nothing was the hardest part for me. I loved creating, but the truth was that nothing was calling. I had to find the courage to face this phase of life I found myself in. Maybe I wasn't being indulgent after all. According to Jaworski, people were more afraid of not having lived than they were of dying. And for me, without that feeling of aliveness, what was the point? I didn't care what it was that I was supposed to do, I just wanted to feel alive again. I didn't realise that many old parts of me had to first die.

I was doing my best to let go of controlling my life. But I was still stuck in the victimised state of relating to life as if it were *happening* to me. Until now, my usual pattern had been to commit to something and then do whatever it took to 'make it happen.' That way came at a cost, though. Exhaustion. And now I simply lacked the energy to push. It was a blessing in disguise. It seemed that my inability to push myself was the only thing that forced me to find a new way.

As my search for answers continued, I came across new ideas about what really mattered in life. Erich Fromm shares in his book *The Art of Living* that 'Love is the only satisfactory answer to the problem of human existence.' Whereas my life had once been guided by my goals, these days I had a greater focus on the quality of my relationships. I no longer believed I was wasting my time by socialising too much and not being as productive as I *should* be. But then, when the fear got too much, I would simply forget all this new loving wisdom. This wisdom, after all, was not going to pay the bills.

So I fell back into feeling indulgent and ashamed of not being able to get my act together. I could not figure out where my old confident self had gone. I wanted her back. Søren Kierkegaard said, "To venture causes anxiety, but not to venture is to lose one's self…And to venture in the highest is precisely to be conscious of one's self." But it did not feel fair that I had to suffer so much just because I dared to venture.

But there seemed to be wisdom in not taking action. I had to simply face the anxiety around not having a clear plan and give up worrying about moving into action. The process of transformation requires us to learn something new. Relating to life from control and the need for certainty did not allow space for anything new to arise, though. Rather than bringing fear to not knowing the answer, my job was to bring curiosity. But this was easier said than done in the face of the darkness that kept threatening my world.

WILL MY CHANCES PASS ME BY?

And then out of nowhere, I was contacted by a recruitment company in the Middle East about a job. My energy shot through the roof with excitement. Initially, I thought the job may be in Dubai given that was where the recruitment company was based. But no. It was in Beirut. I was so excited. All those years of wanting to work in Lebanon, and now there was a chance. And the opportunity came to me. I had not needed to go searching. Well, I didn't have the job yet, but it was great to see that I could still get excited about something. The process of hiring for the role was going to take time, though, as the company was going through many changes. So I had time to consider whether a stable and grounded life in Australia was more important than following exciting opportunities around the world. The job in Lebanon sounded interesting, however, I was concerned that it would take more energy than I had. On the other hand, it could also be a wonderful opportunity to get close to Lebanon, my birthplace. I had to face the fact that I was far from fit and healthy for a senior corporate role. But for now, all I had to do was wait for them to get back in touch when their formal hiring process began.

My thoughts continued. *Why do I feel so pressured, in an unspoken way, to be in a job? Why is there such an expectation that we should know what we want to do in life? Why am I so worried about my inquiry taking so long?* I had a record in my head warning me *You'll go backwards if you don't stay in the workforce, so you'd better not stay out of it for too long.* The pressure to have a career was all around. Subtly and not so subtly.

The biggest shame for me was that I actually had time to enjoy not knowing what I wanted to do with the rest of my life, but my fears always surfaced and got in the way.

Will my chances pass me by? Is a career what I really want? Should I go to an ashram and meditate some more on it? So much noise in my head. I couldn't make it stop.

I started to feel like I was wasting my life with all the heaviness that consumed me. I just wanted to feel a deep joy and gratitude for all that I had. *I can't bear my sad story any longer.* I was tired of the searching, of freaking out. Once again, I fell to my knees. *God, I'm begging you please. I can't keep going this way.*

Was I getting impacted by Dad's illness? I didn't know how I felt about that. I was still in denial. But my feelings of fear did seem to surface around his health issues.

I was desperate for my physical health to get its act together. I wanted my energy back. My low grade fatigue left me feeling like I had the flu all the time. I felt irritated and resentful of so much money spent on my health, and not a single penny coming in. Shame spiraled up around my situation.

My fear had overtaken me.

Does life require such meltdowns in order for us to fully let go? That was the eternal question.

I WANT MY SUPERWOMAN MUM BACK

On a call with Alexander, he told me that I was his rock and he needed me to get healthy and toughen up again. Alexander was going through his own life changes, and he needed me to hurry up and get better. "I want my superwoman mum back," he'd said.

I had little energy to give. But I could hear his need. I understood it. Was that what it was like for my mother when I needed her and she was not there? Barely being able to be in her own body?

I tried to explain to Alexander that I needed to find a new way, as my superwoman ways had caused both of us damage. "Yeah, yeah, I know, but you know what I mean?" he said. I let it go.

Here I was, desperate for my own mummy who had nothing to give, while my son was needing his. He was in his own life enquiry. His own transitioning. I could feel his growing fears. His growing pains. I felt powerless to provide him the solid ground he needed. It broke my heart. We both lashed out at each other in desperation. We both suffered. We were getting to our own rock bottom in our relationship.

Some people get used to you having your act together and get annoyed when you can no longer support them. Other people feel closer to you when you fall apart. They feel more normal around you. They get to see you are not superwoman, you are human. But no matter what, it is hard for others to truly be with someone's deep pain.

Some people would tell me how amazing I was and reassured me that it would all turn out. For some reason, that just made me feel worse. It felt like pressure. As much as I appreciated acknowledgement, constantly being told I was amazing felt like a burden. Positivity on top of agony was simply more agony. I knew they were trying to help, but it didn't. I just needed to be held in the moment, to just be and to have someone be with me, just the way I was. One moment at a time was all I could survive. I could no longer connect one second into the future! It was a one-moment-at-a-time journey, and right then I had nothing to give. Even to my son.

I simply wanted to curl up into the foetal position. The terror had now manifested itself in excruciating physical pain that was lodged so deep inside my chest that I would have images of stabbing it out. Popping it, like an overblown balloon threatening to burst at any minute. I nursed a constant throbbing headache. With all this emotional and physical pain I was experiencing, I found it too hard to stay in my body.

I needed to stop *being* with my anxiety. Instead, I desperately needed to be distracted from it. I couldn't go on living like this. I just wanted relief from the pain. I wanted this to be over. I would have visions of driving my car into oncoming traffic, or better still, a semi-trailer so I could smash the pain up. Every minute of my life now felt like hell.

I started to feel angry with all the mindfulness talk, all that 'Observe your feelings' talk. What did they know about how much it was hurting? It was like telling someone who had their hand chopped off to just be mindful of it.

I knew I needed counselling, but I couldn't even get my act together to find a counsellor. I may have left it too long.

My rescue fantasies returned; I just wanted to be held by an adult. A strong person. Everyone my age I talked to seemed to be going through their own stuff. Their own version of life not working anymore. Overworked, dissatisfied, lonely, blah, blah, blah…

Even at a recent Women's Conference where the speakers were very inspiring and full of energy, I felt the familiar pressure when they used the phrase 'reach your full potential.' See, it was everywhere! I thought back to when I was on the Camino. There, it was not like we were aiming to reach our full potential; we were aiming to reach our *full presence.*

With pain this bad, though, I had only one choice left. *Surrender.*

*

I'd been taking Dad to his radiotherapy sessions. I felt the knots in my stomach tighten as I saw him struggle out of the car. He was too proud to let me help him. I was proud of him for being independent. He never complained and was always positive. It made me feel so small. While he fought for his life, I had lost the will to live.

HAND ME THE DRUGS! I'M BEGGING YOU, PLEASE...

Since I could no longer be in my house alone out in the country, I moved in with my parents in the city where my network was closer. But I did this under the guise of helping Mum support Dad with his cancer. I could not deal with the shame of 'living with my parents' at forty-four years of age. Deep down, I knew it was important not to isolate during such times, but my shame still ran deep.

The fact was that I was worried about *me*. I was in pain, and I could not see a way out all by myself.

In the midst of all this, I somehow managed to find myself in a relationship. I had so little to give and was unaccustomed to receiving. But I had little fight in me, so I allowed myself to be taken care of. And so a relationship began, though it wasn't the strongest foundation for one.

My boyfriend encouraged me to take medication. I would get furious with him. I had been praying for a spiritual awakening. Given my new spiritual teachings, I thought this pain was a necessary pathway to that awakening. I thought if I had enough courage to truly feel my pain I would come out the other end. But he was quite insistent.

He bore the brunt of my spiritual superiority. I even threatened to leave him if he was going to encourage me to use drugs instead of 'working through' my pain. But this was the last stretch of my spiritual superiority. I had to get that I was not above being a human being. So I became willing to discuss it with my doctor. If I'd had any other health problem, I would have been all over it. But I allowed myself to suffer beyond what was healthy.

Having said that, time and time again I would go to the doctor and explain my symptoms and they would sympathise. They knew my dad was dying, so they would suggest that that was the reason for my symptoms. But still, something else felt wrong. Something just didn't make sense. The pain was beyond tolerable. I was still too proud to tell them exactly how bad it was. And I didn't have the words for it.

I'd already had every blood test under the sun. Testing for vitamin deficiencies, hormone imbalances, and thyroid health. But nothing showed up. If only doctors were better trained in detecting the symptoms of anxiety. If only they had been able to point me in the right direction sooner. Or, at a minimum, help me make sense of these crazy making symptoms.

I did feel lucky to have a doctor who pushed more for therapy than drugs, but I found myself saying, *Please, just give me something to ease the pain. I can't take it anymore.* Yes, I was desperate. By this stage, I would have begged for drugs if I had to. Thankfully, he left my dignity intact. He was a gentle combination of care, doctoring, and counselling. His diagnosis? According to a one page questionnaire: depression. But that did not resonate in the slightest with me. With what little energy I had, I argued. I may have become depressed, but I knew myself enough to know that it was anxiety. An extreme version of anxiety. But it mattered little. By then, I didn't believe that anything could help. Not even drugs. But what was there to lose?

In this time of my greatest fragility, I had to choose to not judge myself. And at the same time, I had to let go of my need to 'be evolved' in how I handled my personal transformation. Choosing to take medication for my anxiety was a lesson in humility of the toughest kind.

There is so much stigma around taking medication. Despite having asked for medication once before, I still had my own judgements about using medication to deal with pain. Many a spiritual teacher harshly judged the medical path to treating depression and anxiety. One of those teachers was the leader of a one-day workshop that I had taken. She was wonderful. So clear, so straight. However, she had a strong opinion about all the people who were on medication. She made the joke (but was quite serious) about how all the medication was going into our waterways and our fish were now on Prozac! She mused that we were all on medication because our food supply was contaminated.

It was hard for me to not feel like I was a weak person for taking the medication route. I guess this was where one needed to truly tune into what was right for them. My shame, my feeling weak, my drama around taking medication was the bigger issue. I had a choice. I chose medication. No one was going to reward me for martyring myself in the name of spirituality. Spending my days in agony felt futile.

*

Life was now consumed with appointments with Dad. Our least favourite appointment was with his oncologist, who wore shiny shoes, fancy socks, and had a big desk in his office that separated him from us. He posed in his big, black chair as he spoke in metaphors that dragged on and on. He listened little to my father's request for no chemotherapy. Dad felt pressured. When we left Shiny Shoes' office I reflected Dad's upset back to him. Dad, I was learning, just went quiet when he was upset. On the drive back home, we decided to find a more *human* doctor. At a minimum, Dad needed to feel supported by a warm oncologist. The system did not make this transition easy, but we survived the awkwardness and found a lovely female oncologist Dad immediately felt he could resonate with. She had the warmth Dad needed and made him feel safe.

THE HORROR OF MEDICATION

Nobody prepared me for how bad medication would be in the first few weeks. It got far worse before it got better. The intensity of the terror and dread was a thousand fold. Negative irrational thoughts attacked my mind at such a speed I could not counter them. My heart pounded so hard I thought it would explode out of my chest. No wonder people killed themselves when starting on medication. Thank God for the accompanying sedatives I was given to help calm my now out-of-control nervous system. And thank God for my boyfriend, who rarely left my side.

Was there any escape from this hell?

After three days, it felt like the worst was over. I began to adjust to the horror of medication. My boyfriend and I went up to my house in the country for the weekend. With him by my side, I was able to return home to at least get some respite from seeing Dad fade further away each day.

Once we arrived in the country, I slept for twenty-four hours straight. And then another twenty-four hours. I was exhausted from holding it together for so long. Thanks to my boyfriend, I was watered and fed in bed as I was unable to lift my head off the pillow.

By the end of the weekend, I was a bit more rested, but I had not fully adjusted to the medication yet. Driving back to my parents' place from the country, I thought every car was going to smash into us. The mere stimulation of the car drive was too much for my nervous system to hold. I was just grateful to have my boyfriend behind the wheel and not me. He was always there for me, but I was constantly worried about the imbalance in our relationship and concerned about how he would cope once I got better and became more independent again. I argued against the relationship, given that I had nothing to give, while he argued for the relationship, saying it didn't matter.

INSPIRATION DOES NOT ALWAYS MAKE SENSE

Around this time, I was inquiring into doing a course that focused on writing a book to position my expertise in the market. My head was telling me that perhaps this was something I *should* do. It was a one-year program focused on maximising your earning potential. This program resonated with my head, but not my heart.

Still desperate for some inspiration, my search led me to a one-day writing course. As soon as I landed on the course's website, I felt butterflies in my stomach. For the first time in almost two years I felt inspiration. I had never anticipated my inspiration being about a one-day writing course. When I inquired into the course, there was an immediate resonance with the woman running it. She was light and real. There was no hard sell. None of that artificial professionalism that usually makes me cringe. I was frustrated that I had to wait a few months before the course started.

That one-day course changed the direction of my emotional life. Something new awoke in me.

The workshop didn't disappoint. By now my medication had settled me somewhat. The worst of the terror and dread had subsided. At a minimum, I had resumed the will to live, but anxiety was still my daily companion.

We were given a challenge in the workshop to submit a piece of writing by ten o'clock that night. I had not had a deadline in ages, let alone one that inspired me. I had a busy evening, but I took the challenge on anyway. I knew from my years of coaching that when one committed to something they were inspired by, and then delivered on it against the odds, magic happened.

I loved that rush to make something happen against all odds, especially when inspired. So that night I managed to finish my piece of writing and send it through. That weekend was one of the happiest weekends I'd had in ages. You would have thought I'd conquered the world. I had. But it was my inner world.

I left the course committed to writing this book. I felt a strong desire to trust this inspiration, not knowing what would emerge. Finally, it was not about financial security. It was not about paying the bills. It was about following that deeper knowing, that flutter in my belly that told me I was alive and that life was exciting.

Every other thing I was looking into doing—getting a job, starting my own business—were making sense in my head, but not in my heart. There was no energy there. So when I had a feeling that was so clear to me, I knew I had to follow it, despite it not making any practical sense whatsoever.

I now had a writing mentor, and it felt wonderful. For the first time since leaving work, I felt alive with new purpose. Never did I imagine I would write a book on anxiety, but this was the book I felt called to write. If one person could benefit from reading about my struggle with anxiety, then I knew it would be worth it. I just had to trust that the rest of my life would fall into place. This was not my head talking. I felt this clarity in my whole body.

Why had it taken so long to figure all this out? I was learning this was not a question that helped. But I had learnt that I needed to have more protective layers stripped away from my survivalist identity to be able to hear more deeply what my soul was saying to me, and to listen to where life was now guiding me to go.

The first day I sat down to write this book, my anxiety abated. If that wasn't a sign, what was?

*

There was a new drug on the market that promised a sliver of hope in the treatment of cancer. The only caveat was that Dad had to have at least three rounds of chemotherapy to qualify for this experimental treatment. It was maddening. In Dad's desperation, he agreed to chemotherapy. It ended up trashing Dad's immune system, which was no surprise. And so began endless stints in hospital with no sign of real progress.

The intensity of caring for a parent dying of cancer was unrelenting, even if some days there was nothing to do, and even if many people were on hand to support in every way. I had failed to pay attention to how much Dad's condition was impacting me. And even if I did, I wouldn't have changed a thing. He was still a welcome respite from myself.

HIGH OCTANE IS BACK

With the help of medication, I slowly returned to a semblance of my old self. But this time something had changed. I no longer felt that I needed to have goals that were impressive or ones that made me feel safe. I just wanted to feel alive. I wanted to be consumed by a project that gave me life, and for some strange reason, writing this book seemed to be consuming me in the best possible way.

I maintained a routine to keep me grounded emotionally. I had lots of energy; I would wake early to get to work at my writing desk. It was a foreign feeling. It felt a bit manic, though, as if my High Octane-self was back. That feeling I had always been so addicted to. But I was still not getting enough deep sleep. A side effect of my medication.

Whereas once I could barely get through looking at my emails, I now found myself interested in creating rhythms and routines that supported me. The future seemed bright. I now stayed on top of emails, had an impeccable space, and this new energy was having me rip through all my things that needed to be done on the property. I was moved to spring clean my room in Melbourne, wash my car, then Mum's car, and still have energy to drive down to the country where I felt like doing even more work. I loved having energy.

I still felt that I was not all the way there yet, but I had turned a corner. *Exhale.*

This newfound sense of wellbeing and what seemed to be a change in personality presented a problem for my relationship. My boyfriend had been there for me in my darkest time, but even though I was now loving life again and capable of caring for myself, he continued to treat me like I was still sick. He loved to take care of me, but now that I was stronger and making progress, his attention made me feel thwarted and weak instead of cared for. My attention was on Dad and getting my life together. His attention was on me. I needed space. He needed connection. The foundation of our relationship had been shaky to begin with, and now it was cracking. Before long we had to face the fact that the timing was simply not right, so we parted ways. I regretted not being strong enough to trust my instincts in the first place. The impact was high.

THE HANGOVER

On the other side of my High Octane-self, I was finding that I needed to be more quiet and silent than ever before. It was the only way I found I could really hear myself. There was a deep desire at times to have the space and support to drop deeply into my pain and to work out what the source of it really was. But then I remembered how bad it felt and figured, *Thank God for drugs.*

I eventually came off my high from the last few days, which resulted in a really good night's sleep. It was hard to contain myself during my highs. As a result of these manic highs, I reduced my dose in hope of more balance. I was also still experiencing chest pains, to a lesser extent, as well as a constant low grade headache. Just as I got excited about having energy and enthusiasm, my anxiety would return. Sedatives were still part of my daily routine. They soothed my chest pains and headaches. Thankfully, the worst of the dread and fear were still at bay. With recovery still in its early days, I continued to fear the darkness would return.

After three days of no deep sleep, I was exhausted. I felt like just laying in bed all day and staring at the ceiling. Couldn't I just get back to normal? I was back to feeling overwhelmed by what little I had going on.

Perhaps Dad coming back home from hospital was affecting me. I noticed Mum had that edge in her voice. It wasn't easy to watch Dad get so thin and to have to look after him day in, day out.

There was so much to focus on. My emotional health, (I refused to call it mental health; it made me feel like a nutter, which I knew I was not), Dad being sick, Alexander needing support, me not knowing what I wanted to do with my life, and not feeling strong enough for full-time work. It felt like a lot to hold. Too much, at times.

I fantasised about the day when I would be able to get up and not have to face any anxiety. A time when I could feel joy and just flow with my day. I could taste it coming my way. I tried to keep my faith.

SENTENCED TO SUPPLEMENTS

At least my medication was now allowing my appetite to return, so I figured it was time to start getting my health back in order. For months I had had little appetite and had lost a lot of weight. Still struggling with my emotions, I had little motivation to care about healthy eating and knew I needed support. So I went to a naturopath my mother recommended. I also wanted support to get off medication. I knew my body was still not strong enough, though, so that is where I put my focus.

When I first got to my naturopath I was exhausted and still living with a mild constant headache. I had been going to the gym for three months and was now physically stronger, however, I was still exhausted. She ran many a thorough test. All the tests my doctor would deem unscientific. The diagnosis? Leaky gut, fatty liver, inflammation, infection, and hormonal imbalance. Basically, I was told that I had a highly toxic body that required rebuilding from the inside out.

Her regime was thorough. I had asked for help and some structure, and I got it! My new regime became a full time job. My list of supplements included an intestinal flush, magnesium, selenium, zinc, special tea, flaxseed oil, evening primrose oil, iodine, cognitex, vitamin D3, potassium phosphate and magnesium phosphate, brown rice protein, glutagenics, prebiotic, basica alkalizer, detox kit homeopathics, living greens superfood, CoQ10, 500C methoxy, neuro A, Vitamin B12, essential oils for balance, positivity, and purpose, and a special diet that helped clean my system. Each visit to the naturopath cost a small fortune, but I was willing to do anything to get my health back. I felt great, but my life was now run by supplements, and I became afraid to live without them. No wonder people chose medication. It was much cheaper. My medication cost me five dollars a month by comparison to hundreds each visit.

I found myself spending all of my money on my health. A not-so-exciting prospect. Not only did I look forward to getting off my medication, I began to look forward to living a life without being reliant on supplements for energy.

Despite getting my energy back, feeling great, and now being on the lowest dose of my medication, I started to feel like I was going to be sentenced to living on supplements and a strict diet for the rest of my life. The thought of it felt so depressing. There had to be a middle road to getting my health back.

Thankfully, new answers began to emerge, albeit slowly.

GAD: GENERALISED ANXIETY DISORDER

I was resisting the language the doctors used to diagnose my condition. GAD, or Generalised Anxiety Disorder. What a nondescript, benign medical term. I had no affinity with the term whatsoever. But I wanted relief from this hell, and I needed answers, so having a diagnosis to research provided direction. I wondered if my feelings were related to Dad having cancer? I was sure the emotional strain added to my feelings, but something told me there was more to it. My inner dialogue rarely stopped: *How could this happen to me? Why is this happening to me? Is it the burden of modern day living? Is it the emptiness of no longer being a mother? Is it a fear of returning to the corporate world and getting stuck? Is it loneliness? Is it my ancestral pain? Am I ignoring something?*

I didn't know, but I had to find out. The term 'disorder' challenged me the most, but in time, I learnt the distinction between anxiety and anxiety disorder. Anxiety was a normal response to a specific, stressful event. The anxiety usually subsided once the event was resolved or had passed. Anxiety disorder, on the other hand, continued regardless of whether the event was present or not, eventually resulting in disruption to normal living. So I became clear that I was struggling with anxiety disorder given that I was no longer able to be with the terror that had gripped me, and I could no longer function the way I used to be able to.

And by now, I had well and truly manifested many of the physical symptoms that accompanied anxiety disorder: acute chest pain, constant headaches, neck tension, fear of impending doom, inability to rest, insomnia, exhaustion, flu-like symptoms, and most importantly, feeling like I was going crazy.

So despite the shame that accompanied the term 'disorder' for me, I conceded. I had anxiety disorder. But anxiety and anxiety disorder were often used interchangeably, causing confusion for those who didn't have that distinction, including me.

A TIRED BRAIN: FEAR OF FEAR

A friend of my mother had passed on a book recommendation. It was a book on agoraphobia by a woman named Dr. Claire Weekes. Now, if the term 'anxiety disorder' did not repel me enough, the term 'agoraphobia' certainly did. For that reason I took my time looking into Dr. Weekes. But eventually, I looked her up. It turned out that Dr. Weekes was well known internationally for her special understanding of the treatment of what she referred to as 'nervous fatigue'; she was also nominated for the Nobel Prize for Medicine in 1989 for her work.

Understanding, she said, was the forerunner of cure. Dr. Weekes suggested that nervous fatigue manifested in one or more ways. It begins with muscular fatigue, which is akin to how someone would feel after a workout, but you experience the fatigue from the smallest exertion of effort. For some, this can creep in slowly over a long period of time. For others, it can be caused by a specific stressful event such as a surgical operation or an accident. Sleep doesn't come easy for those suffering from muscular fatigue, and often, no amount of sleep provides the deep rest that is needed. This resonated deeply with me. I finally understood why my last house move felt so hard and why no amount of sleep was leaving me refreshed or energised.

Next, emotional fatigue sets in. With the body now drained of energy, it has little resilience against what used to be normal events. This results from the brain being 'over-sensitised' from an overproduction of adrenaline to the brain. With the brain being constantly bathed in adrenaline, heightened sensitivity ensues. Simply speaking, the brain is tired and highly sensitive, causing the slightest event to trigger and re-trigger the nervous system. Like a gun firing off at the slightest invitation. This sensitisation is the main cause of emotional fatigue, depleting emotional energy.

Bewilderment (feeling like you are going crazy) and fear often accompany emotional fatigue, keeping it alive. Bewilderment, Dr. Weekes wrote, 'works by keeping a sensitised person under the constant strain of asking, *why am I like this, what is this thing that is happening to me, why can't I be my old self.* [S]he looks at others and then thinks, *why can't I be like them?* And if [s]he finds no answers to his[her] questions, fear comes into the picture. Fear of the state [s]he is in.' With every word I read, the tight grip of feeling like I was going crazy began to loosen. Her words echoed my own crazy making thoughts, almost verbatim.

She further validated my experience by saying that bewilderment can drive anxiety sufferers to spend days, weeks, or even years looking for answers that might bring an end to their feeling of going crazy. She explained that by adding bewilderment and fear, the already sensitised person keeps themselves in a cycle of fear-adrenaline-fear, producing the very symptoms of stress that the person fears. So the cycle goes on. It was reassuring to hear that what drives anxiety sufferers the most crazy is their inability to describe their own symptoms to themselves, let alone to those who have never had such an experience. Slowly, slowly, my sanity was being restored.

Next, mental fatigue sets in. The mere act of thinking, not to mention speaking, starts to require effort. This was around the time I unconsciously began to isolate myself. During that time, I could not shake my irrational worries. Eventually, my negative thoughts began to stick like glue. My sensitised brain amplified them and made them real, when all the while they were simply silly thoughts in my now exhausted brain. As I dealt with the onslaught of endless negative thoughts, I began to experience what Dr. Weekes calls spiritual fatigue. My world had become a kind of hell from which I dreamt to escape.

Dr. Weekes says that few people recognise these fatigues given they accumulate in such a gradual way, and often in this order.

If not recognised early enough, nervous fatigue eventually develops into 'nervous illness.' This is when people get stuck in the cycle of adrenaline-fear-adrenaline and then become fearful of their constant state of fear. The 'fear of fear' is what causes the nervous illness, which was Dr. Weekes' term for anxiety disorder.

I distinctly remember the shift from having feelings of fear to starting to fear my state of fear, as if it would never end. As if this was going to be what the rest of my life would feel like. According to Dr. Weekes, this 'fear of fear' is what robs us of hope. This then adds adrenaline to an already tired brain, further entrenching the experience of confusion and feeling like we are going crazy. So, as the stress increases, so does the body's erratic and more involuntary behaviour.

Recovery from anxiety disorder was not rocket science for Dr. Weekes. She did not advise a therapeutic approach, or to search out for the root cause of anxiety. Rather, she advised 100 percent acceptance of how you were feeling. This was a relief to me as I had spent years on the couch and found little motivation to go back there. Now that the medication was taking some effect, I was more capable of taking on the practice of 100 percent acceptance—just like all my spiritual textbooks told me, just like the practice of mindfulness suggested.

But why was I able to believe this when Dr. Weekes talked to me this way? Well, as she said, understanding was *the forerunner of cure*. And finally, I was beginning to understand.

How could it be that I had to search for so long before I found such simple answers? Why did my doctors not explain this to me? Why didn't our Australian mental health hotline explain this to me? I had reached out for telephone counselling, but all I got was a pat on the back and that this was normal given all the changes in my life. I felt so angry that such simple information was not being dished out by every doctor and mental health institution in town.

For now, though, I was thankful to have this new understanding which was finally pulling me out of my sense of going crazy. I finally realised that there was nothing *wrong* with me—I had simply overloaded my nervous system with adrenaline from all of my years of striving and trying to prove myself, rendering me hyper-sensitive to the slightest thought or event.

This new understanding further soothed the shame I felt about my anxiety disorder. It also gave me words to explain to others what I was dealing with.

Dr. Weekes felt like the mother whose womb I could climb into for that safe space, her words instantly calming me. Soothing me.

*

Dad was back in hospital, and I called to tell him we were on our way to get him his favorite food. He said he had to fast for a CT scan and asked if we could bring food later. And then he started to apologise for inconveniencing us. I told him not to worry, that we would just make it work. Then there was a silence, and I thought we'd been disconnected. I could not understand or hear him, until I realised he was sobbing on the phone.

When I got to hospital, I sat next to Dad. He rubbed my back gently and said he felt so guilty always asking us to do things. I reassured him that it was my privilege. I asked him if he wanted me to rub his feet. He said yes. I was so touched, gut wrenched, and so full of love at the same time. It was such a sacred space to be there for someone who was getting so close to death.

So when I was finally contacted about the job in Beirut, the one that had, months ago, left me wondering if I would accept or decline, my decision was easy and clear. I declined. I just couldn't leave Dad in his last few months. This was where I needed to be.

ANXIETY IS NOT A MENTAL ILLNESS: RECOVERY IS TOTALLY POSSIBLE

Not only did I have an aversion to the term 'anxiety disorder', I had an even bigger aversion to anxiety being referred to as a mental illness. As if there was actually something wrong with my brain or intelligence.

The Anxiety Centre states that 'Anxiety is NOT a disease, illness, or biological condition you inherit or contract. It's also not a result of a chemical imbalance or biological problem in the brain.' Anxiety, they suggested, was the result of certain kinds of apprehensive behaviours, most notably worry. A behaviour that can be turned around. They explained that although anxiety affected the body in real biochemical ways, it originated from our thinking, and both aspects needed to be addressed for a lasting recovery.

Dr. Weekes also referred to anxiety as a thinking illness. An illness of your attitude towards fear. The fear of the constant fear. The fact that anxiety is caused by how one thinks and behaves was good news. It meant that recovery was totally possible.

*

Dad was feeling a bit stronger after recovering from yet another blood transfusion. Now the question was whether or not the new treatment was helping. We were hoping Dad would make it to my younger sister's wedding in February the following year, which was four and a half months away. We silently knew it would take a miracle. My sister was distraught about this, but Dad had insisted that she not bring the wedding forward. He was still in denial about how sick he was. It was hard to wrap my own mind around it, too. The doctors were no longer commenting on how long he would live for, but the uncertainty for my little sister was difficult. Still, none of us had the heart to push around the issue of the wedding. My heart broke for my sister. She so wanted Dad to walk her down the aisle and couldn't bear the idea of even thinking of a back up plan.

THE TURNING POINT

I had not been working for almost two years now and was wondering out loud to my mum if I should rent my house out. "Do you absolutely have to right now?" Mum asked. "No, not absolutely," I answered. "Then don't," she said. Mum was great like this. Not for one day did Mum put pressure on me to work out my life. She did this effortlessly because it was her gift. She had never been driven to have a career or to be 'successful.' So it really gave me the space to not rush into decisions when I just couldn't. It was not always easy between us. Mum could give me space, but it was too painful for her to be with and hear about my anxiety. And with my dad dealing with cancer, she had even less capacity.

I wondered if I should go and spend time at an ashram, but I didn't want to tuck myself away in a safe environment. There was a part of me that knew clearly that I needed to be in the world and deal with my life. I had escapist thoughts about going on another Camino walk, but then I knew at some point I would need to come back home. These days, I could recognise my running away strategies. So I stayed put.

When we put out to the universe that we are committed to finding a new way to live life, we don't know how life will teach us how to do this. I don't believe that the universe sent me crippling anxiety to teach me a lesson, though. The universe for me is all loving. However, it was my ignoring the signs, not trusting my heart enough, and instead, using my head to make decisions that drove me down to my knees. That was what helped strip away my arrogance. My shame around looking messy. Thinking that I had to have it all handled was my biggest delusion.

*

There were harrowing moments whilst caring for Dad. One day, I walked into hospital and Dad was sitting in a chair shivering and in agony. I could not warm him up. I was trying to be with him in the midst of his physical pain. At one point, I could not stand it anymore and started crying. I could not see him in so much pain. He was so stubborn. All he asked for was two Panadols for his pain. I ran out of his room crying like a hysterical woman asking for stronger pain killers. Morphine, for God's sake. My dad should not have to suffer.

It took time for them to get permission from a doctor to release the morphine. It felt like forever. He was in agony. Given his newfound connection to God, I suggested that we just pray together. There we were, curled up into each other, feeling like the minutes were hours. Thankfully, the morphine arrived and eventually kicked in.

By then, I had managed to both pray with Dad and call every member of my family and ask them to come to hospital immediately. I was a raving mess. I ordered him to never do that to me again and to ask for morphine the second the pain reared its head. I knew he would do it for me. For some reason asking for morphine made him feel weak. Like admitting that he was going to die. A thought he refused to entertain. A thought that evoked terror in him. A thought that not long ago was my only avenue for relief.

Dad was now deteriorating. We were constantly in and out of hospital, and he could no longer be left alone. His need for care increased. But Mum and I found a way to work well together. We had lots of extra support that we could not have done without. My uncle Lee was back in the fold of our lives, rarely leaving Dad's side. For my uncle, this was simply his duty. Dad was his brother, after all.

Just as we got Dad settled back home after a two-week stint in hospital, I woke to him shivering and running a high temperature, which, when undergoing chemotherapy, was a sign of infection. We had to constantly monitor his temperature during this time as it required immediate readmission. It was 4:00 a.m., and the prospect of sending him back to hospital was devastating to me, let alone to Dad. Before, when he'd been in hospital, they dealt with his temperature with Panadol first to see if it abated. So, with the agreement of the hospital nurse, we tried that. Dad refused to go back to hospital. He said, "Let's wait till morning." I respected his wishes. It was a risk, but he was entitled to some of his own decision making.

I woke up around 7:00 a.m. I went to check on him, and thankfully, his temperature had completely normalised. It was such a relief. Hospital averted for the day. As much as Dad's condition threw out any plans I had most days, supporting him made my life feel real and fulfilling, as if I had really lived.

HELPING MY SON ACCEPT WHERE I AM

My relationship with Alexander was still strained. But one day, as if by the grace of God, Alexander and I seemed to come to a very clear conclusion about our relationship. Something had to give on both ends. There were truths we both had to hear. When all was said and done, my only request was, "Say anything, but please remember I need love and kindness to be able to hear you." It turned out that Alexander also needed me to be more gentle with him. This became the new foundation for our relationship.

Whilst growing up, Alexander often had to remind me that he was not a coaching client. He was my son. My ways of being practical and factual were not always useful when all he needed was to be held and to be empathised with. Alexander had always been my greatest teacher, but this transition was our hardest.

One of the biggest challenges I faced was supporting my son in his life while needing him to understand my current limitations. I mistakenly believed that my job as a mother was done given Alexander was now twenty-two, but I was fast learning that now, more than ever, my parenting counted. I felt his fear of not having his mother around physically, and now emotionally, to be his rock whilst he transitioned into manhood. I wanted to find a way of describing what I was going through whilst letting him know I could totally be there for him, too. Maybe not exactly how he would like it to look, but I was capable of full emotional support now that the worst of my anxiety was over.

I didn't want him to treat me like I was broken, because I wasn't entirely broken. Only a part of me was. I likened it to a broken leg. And I reassured him that it would heal; I would get the chance to feel like a good mother again.

And so began a new relationship between us. One based on mutual respect and kindness.

*

The chemotherapy and other treatment were not working. Chances of survival were now slim. We didn't have the heart to tell Dad that he only had months. He was fading before our eyes.

I bathed him three times a week, quickly getting over the fact that I had to see my father naked. Rather than it be embarrassing, it was touching. Such an intimate space had deepened between us. I wished I could completely switch off the part of my brain that believed I should be doing anything other than being there supporting Dad, so I could fully embrace the gift that it was. But that was not so easy. So I did my best to juggle both. The need to get somewhere and the desire to be fully present with him, so close to the edge of life and death. And finally, so close to my Dad. What we have in common is our inability to sit still for too long. Cancer brought him to his knees, anxiety brought me to mine.

AN EPIDEMIC UNDIAGNOSED

Whilst doing my research for this book, I was shocked to learn about the statistics on anxiety. My exposure to mental health from the media and even the workplace was dominated by the topic of depression. However, the Australian Bureau of Statistics concluded as far back as 2008 that, 'Anxiety is the most common emotional condition, outranking depression and possibly drug and alcohol abuse.' And, according to the Anxiety and Depression Association of America, 'Anxiety disorders are the most common mental illness in the U.S., affecting 40 million adults age eighteen and older, or 18.1 percent of the population every year.' Some suggest that the percentage is much higher given how many people go undiagnosed even when seeking out support. Many do not seek any support at all, and worse still, some of us don't even know we have issues with anxiety. Paul Foxman, in his book *Dancing with Fear,* suggests that 75 percent of anxiety sufferers receive no help at all.

With all this, was it any wonder I went undiagnosed for so long? And was it any wonder the doctors went straight for the depression diagnosis rather than properly diagnosing me with anxiety and fully explaining it to me?

A NECESSARY CRISIS

Although my anxiety felt like it had come out of nowhere, I was learning that there was more often than not a lead up to it. It had not occurred to me that what I had come to consider normal in my life was far from normal for my nervous system. The multiple stressors of work, travel, surgery, and parental demands were cumulative and overloaded my nervous system, especially given that I rarely allowed sufficient recovery. Even during my one year off, I had multiple projects with very little 'doing nothing' time. The thought of taking time off work without having a plan or any projects to focus on was far too terrifying for me, but my inability to stop and relax proved to have the same effect anyway.

There also appeared to be a propensity to anxiety given certain childhood experiences, where one's personality begins to take shape. My good girl act required me to master the art of hypervigilance of staying in tune with my mother's needs and what might keep her happy. Despite my strategy leaving me feeling safe, I was in a constant state of high alert.

This trait had its upside. It allowed me to be in tune with other people, which served me in my career and with coaching, but I didn't have an 'off' switch, and I often ignored my own needs. It was no accident I chose coaching as a career.

My childhood training as little counsellor also assisted with my success.

For most of my career, I barely took a day off work when I was sick. I had bought into the 'soldier on' attitude, relying on Panadol to get me through a headache or any flu I might be fighting off. I was impatient with myself, unaware of my 'just get over it' mechanism. I had to succeed no matter what. I lived my life ignoring the signs my body was giving me. I lived on a diet of *shoulds* and *someday, one day*. I kept trying to control my environment to avoid fear and sought security instead. I worked hard to be highly competent and dependable, holding myself to the highest standards, believing if I achieved them, I'd feel safe. I have always had difficulty relaxing. I constantly felt agitated. Restless. Impatient and tense. Burying myself in activity. I was certainly not enjoying life, except for a sense of gratification in my accomplishments. My propensity for perfectionism had me push myself harder just to prove myself, further elevating my stress levels. I did not heed the warning of 'I need rest' when I first took time off work. I reacted to how much rest I actually needed. I began to fear my fatigue, thinking I would never recover. So I pushed on, even if to a lesser extent. With my low levels of energy, I found it hard to burn through my agitation. I had to learn to be with it. To allow it. But the lessons were hard. I was coming to the conclusion that embracing my fears and learning to allow them, rather than react to them, was what there was to learn. For me, anxiety was a signal, a message that my life was out of balance and that change was needed. Anxiety became my necessary crisis.

*

My mum could not bring herself to tell my father that the new treatment was not working, but she knew he had to be told. I was now extremely close to Dad, so I agreed to be the one to tell him. It was delicate. As he digested the information, he slipped into another world, but then snapped back.

"Where did you go just now?" I asked him.

"I don't know," he answered. "But I'm not scared."

A peace as pure as a newborn baby sleeping descended on the room around us. I have no words to describe the beauty of such a moment.

But then fear would return.

I had needed a break and drove down to the country for a few days. My mother and little sister held the fort. Dad was now in hospital full-time. Dad seemed to be quickly going downhill, becoming delirious. My mum and sister were lighthearted about it all, so I was not expecting to see what I saw when I was summoned back to Melbourne less than a week later. Dad had been moved into full-time palliative care. I walked into his room and saw him in a completely vegetative state. The shock was a bit too much. He had visitors, so to get a semblance of privacy, I quickly made my way to the bathroom and broke down and sobbed. We expected to lose him within days.

What followed was an onslaught of visitors, the new palliative care facility unable to tame the Lebanese herd that rarely left Dad's side. As each cousin eagerly came to visit, they would walk into Dad's room and then, as quickly as possible, walk out in shock and tears.

And then, as if from out of nowhere, Dad regained his senses. The doctors had found the right dose of psychotic drugs to keep him stable. There was renewed hope for him to hang on until the wedding. For now, we were glad that he had defied the odds and made it until Christmas. On Christmas Day, Dad showed little interest in having his children and grandchildren around him, which triggered old wounds. It was hard to reconcile these emotions given that we had no right to expect anything of our dying father.

But before long, Dad was out and about, unable to sit still in palliative care. Someone had told him that palliative care was where people get sent to die, which is true, but this drove Dad into a bit of a frenzy. Uncle Lee was assigned the role of full-time chauffeur by now, and who was my uncle to argue with a dying man? My uncle was already grieving the fact that he was going to lose his best friend and lamenting the years lost to silly sibling fighting, so he gave his all while he still could. But then one day, as Dad was getting up from the table at Uncle Lee's restaurant, he fell. His hip had broken.

A BRICK CAME OFF MY CHEST

It was now a choice between having Dad live with a broken hip or having a very risky hip operation that had little chance of success.

I went to visit Dad the night before his operation. I arrived late after visiting hours and was watching the Australian Open tennis tournament with him. He was in good spirits, believing all would go well with his operation. Then a young nurse came in and told me I had to leave. Visiting hours were over. I told her I needed to stay with Dad a bit longer; I could not exactly say to her in front of Dad that I knew it would most likely be the last time I got this time with him. Okay, there was a tone in my voice, but when she threatened me with security, I lost my shit. My Dad very calmly said to her, "No need to be such a bitch, dear." Oh, how he could make me laugh. "Don't worry about her," he told me, "she won't do anything."

But on this particular night I could not hold back. I followed her outside, and in front of all her colleagues gave her a piece of my mind, making sure to load her up with all the guilt of a daughter needing to spend time with her dying father. She, understandably embarrassed, told me she hadn't known. I retorted with, "It's your job to know. Instead of lording over me, why don't you attend to doing your job?" I had lost complete control. I had humiliated her, but it did not feel good. In hindsight, I knew I could have handled it better. I felt regretful. I never got the chance to sort that conversation out. So I had to forgive myself.

Dad did not fare well after the operation. He got through one day, but by the next day we, as a family, were called into the hospital to meet with the medical team. It would be a matter of days now. They made space for us to sleep in the hospital from then on.

My sister-in-law saw how tired I was and suggested that I sleep at her place that night and then go to the hospital in the morning. But sleep now was a waste of time. I was on constant high alert with Dad's condition changing by the day. That night I chose to sleep in the hospital. My older sister was there with me as well. Mum, having spent the night in hospital the night before, went home to try to get some rest.

It was midnight when the nurse came in and suggested I call in the rest of the family, just in case Dad didn't make it till the morning. So I did. We each found a place to curl up and go to sleep in the hospital. At 5:00 a.m. we were woken from a restless sleep. Dad was refusing his oxygen, choosing his own time to let go. We gathered. Myself, my mum, my two sisters, and my auntie surrounding him. I called my brother, and he got to say goodbye to Dad over the phone.

A final tear escaped my Dad's eye as he finally passed away. I thanked God for being able to be there with him. The energy was palpable. It was a privilege to be with him as he left his body.

As Dad took his final breath and let go, somehow so did I. The brick that had almost permanently resided on my chest for the past six months lifted. I could breathe freely again. Dad was at peace. And a new kind of peace descended on me. I could not have expected it, but I was floating as if in heaven for days after my dad's death.

In my heightened state of euphoria, I decided that it was time to come off medication, despite the advice of my therapist to stay on it for at least three months after Dad's death. Before long, the euphoria turned into relief. I floated some more. It was easy for me to conclude that my anxiety had been triggered by my Dad's ill health. So I went ahead and immediately began to wean myself off without consulting my doctor.

Then came the day of my Dad's funeral. I wanted more time to just sit with Dad, but the church refused my request. I could not believe it. Not only was my father taken away from us the second he died for a coroner's inquest to ensure there was no foul play given Dad's broken hip, now the church had some rule against any further viewings. They had to get permission from the Vatican, I was told. Seriously! The funeral director, in an attempt to satisfy my request, suggested I spend some time with Dad in the hearse in the car park. I gratefully passed on that offer. The thought of it felt like a bad scene in a movie.

So I let it go.

Dad's funeral service was huge. The church was packed. I knew my Dad was popular, but I had no idea what a good friend he was to so many. As people passed by, giving their condolences at the end of the service, I was shocked by how many people made a point of saying, "He was a good friend."

We then had a wake that was more akin to a party. We chose a pub close to the cemetery. My older sister handled the menu. In honour of Dad making a mean meat pie and having flipped endless hamburgers, my sister made sure both of those items made it onto the menu. The wake was a huge family and cousin reunion. Dad may not have received 'Father of the Year' award, but he could easily have received 'Uncle of the Year' award. The cousins, especially my male cousins, loved him.

Now we had a wedding to prepare for. My sister was getting married in two weeks. We all had to switch gears to make sure my sister got her special day.

I AM RAGE: COMING OFF MEDICATION

Within three weeks of Dad's death I'd come off medication. As was my habit, I went into my 'getting shit done' mode to avoid really feeling. Not only feeling my dad's loss, but just feeling and really listening to myself.

I'd been gripped by rage since my dad passed. There was a reason my therapist suggested waiting three months after Dad died before I stopped my medication. But I didn't listen. I had a strong urge to just get off them.

This rage of mine felt involuntary. I found myself wandering around my house in the country, speaking my rage to myself. I felt like a raving lunatic. Then I had to channel some of the murderous rage in a healthy way, so I took to pruning my forest trees. And I was mumbling my rage to the trees. At times I felt stupid; at other times, I had to tell myself to let it all out. It was becoming clear to me how much I had pushed down, swallowed, over spiritualised. Or maybe this really was one of the symptoms of coming off medication.

I had been ignoring what my feelings were telling me. They were a gentle nudge, telling me that I was heading in the wrong direction. But old habits die hard. I went back to my 'survive at any cost' and just pushed my feelings down. But there was that deeper knowing that this was not the answer. There was another way. I ignored it. I took on too much, and before I knew it, just six months later, I was in a full blown relapse. I didn't think it was possible to ever feel that bad again, but my relapse came with brutal force.

RELAPSE

Being driven was like an addiction. Using my head to make decisions that made sense to my old self was a bad habit that still hung around. I was so frustrated with how long it had taken to get my energy back, that as soon as I had it, I felt like I had to make up for lost time. Like I had to make something of myself.

I thought I was providing the right environment for myself by living in the countryside. Having lots of time in the garden. My tight chest had gone. My confidence had returned. Dad had died, but I barely gave myself time to grieve his loss. I didn't know how to. So I got focused on work. It was what I did best. It was my safe space. Or so I thought.

I was feeling so proud of myself for being off medication and managing my life quite well.

In time, a malaise began to come over me. I was back to being functional in my life but not exactly thrilled with it. My work picked up. Things were coming to me. It felt like the financial tide had turned.

However, I also distinctly remember the deep lack of satisfaction I felt with each new consulting contract I received. I started to wonder if I was choosing the right path. The fear around completely stepping away from my profession was too high. It was what I knew and what I was good at. I knew that there was still a contribution I could make in the world, but I had yet to line up with something that left me feeling alive. Even writing my book, which I had been so inspired about, began to take second place. I found myself thinking of work all the time. Getting anxious about my upcoming workshops. This was a familiar feeling, but I reasoned that I had to pay the bills.

As if amnesia had descended upon me, my driven ways returned. What happened to all that I had learnt about how to deal with anxiety? That anxiety disorder was the fear of fear. What about keeping my nervous system supported and relaxed? What about trying to slow down? I just took on too much, too soon.

I had not wanted to face the fact that I was simply not well enough to ramp up so quickly. I was afraid of yet another year of doing 'not enough.' And I had not trusted my heart or my intuition and made decisions that made me feel safe rather than alive or nourished.

Terrified that I would feel as bad as I once had felt, I called my therapist. Should I get back on medication? Would that be weak? Would it get in the way of my inner work? I wanted permission to take medication. I still related to it as a weakness. *I should have a handle on this by now.*

The sentence that alleviated my sense of failure was when she said, "It seems like your body is letting you down." We discussed how I could support myself with a small dose of medication whilst the stress was a little higher than usual given this new ramp up phase with working again. She was gentle, not judgemental.

So with fear and a sense of weakness guiding my path, I chose to go back on medication before things got too bad. I had forgotten how painful and terrifying the first few weeks of taking medication was.

My second relapse felt like it was double the impact of my first descent into hell. The chest pains and headaches were gone, but the fear was amplified. I did not imagine that there could be a deeper hell.

MY MIND WON'T STOP TERRORISING ME

This time, my brother and his wife scooped me up into their life and took care of me. My brother insisted that I didn't go home and be alone. I was so grateful to both of them.

I had a rough night's sleep. I kept listening to Eckhart Tolle to calm myself and focus on something other than my mind. The thoughts were back. *This will never end. I will never get my confidence back. I think I need to cancel my upcoming workshop. I can't cope. What I have to offer is not that good. It has all been done before. Others seem to be able to get their act together better than me. What is wrong with me? Why me?*

My body kept shaking. I couldn't eat. I could barely drink a sip of water. Within four weeks, I had lost seven kilos. I managed to make it to yoga, and I felt calm in that space...until I thought of life again. *It is all too much. I feel so alone. No one can save me but me. But I don't even feel like I can save me. Is this what the rest of my life is going to look like? I can't take much more of this. I feel like I am letting people down. I'm behind on work.*

I screamed at God. I begged, and tried to soothe myself *It hasn't been a week yet. The medication hasn't had a chance to kick in. Be patient, Cindy. Everything is going to be alright. This, too, shall pass. You are lucky to have a brother and sister-in-law to turn to.*

And so my mind would go.

But once again, death felt like it was the only escape from this hell. To be right back in the same place, where each waking moment was filled with unabating fear, was a blow to my belief that I would ever return to normal. I thought I had changed. I was eating really well. I was supplementing to make sure I did not get sick. I prayed. I meditated. I exercised. I structured my day. I lived in a serene environment. I had friends and family who loved me. I read, I breathed. I had acupuncture. I had healing chiropractic sessions. Yes, things were ramping up, but why this again?

Back to ground zero. Rather, *below* ground zero.

But I was not one to give up. I knew deep in my soul that there was a solution to this recurring terror. And let's face it—even when I was not experiencing terror, I felt like nothing I was doing really made me happy. I was living a functional, terror-free life, but there was an absence of joy. That joy I had experienced when I first took time off work. Where was that joy? I wanted it back.

THERE IS NO MAP

It had taken me almost three years to gain some understanding around what had happened to me. I had chosen a spiritual path, but I had no idea what taking that path really meant. I took on that journey from a kind of ego-centred superiority not realising what the path would unravel. Despite my initial egoic reason for starting this journey, my deeper yearning for feeling more whole, and living from love rather than fear, was taking over. Little did I know that part of that journey included facing the fear and shame that had been masked by all my external accomplishments.

Finally, I had come to the realisation that everything that had motivated me in life up until then was in order to look good, boost my self worth, or avoid feeling pain. I had heard all this before, but now it was sinking in on a visceral level.

One early morning, as I was dealing with the depths of despair yet again, I turned to my soothing practice of listening to spiritual teachings. On this particular morning, I listened to Adyashanti's *The End of Your World*. As you do when you feel like dying. He illuminated ever so clearly what was going on for me. He talked about how the ego's motivation is self-centred: "It's what I want, what I don't want, what can I achieve, who can love me, how much joy can I get, how much happiness can I get, how much unhappiness can I avoid, can I get the right job, can I find the right lover, will I get enlightened?" He refers to all of these things as self-centred motivations.

I was in pursuit of waking up and living a more conscious life—a path I would never have taken had I known how terrifying it could be! However, I was also learning that as I started to wake up to my deeper yearnings, many of my past drivers no longer propelled me forward. I could understand this, but still related to it as if there was something wrong. With me. As if I was now wasting my life by not accomplishing as much as I knew I intellectually could. And not having as 'amazing' a life as I should.

I stopped knowing how to navigate my life. I was still out at sea with nothing to cling to.

At a minimum, I had realised that all those things that I thought would bring me joy, no longer could. It was not like I'd had some spiritual moment in which I woke up; I just saw that my life was not working. What had driven me to 'succeed' had actually hurt me, so that was how I came to lose interest in all my old motivations. I was just too exhausted to pretend that I was someone I wasn't, or to try to impress anyone with my accomplishments. I was also exhausted by all my 'trying to figure it all out.'

I wanted a map of how to find some solid ground again, but I knew full well that there was no step one, two, three. Damn it. I had to learn a new kind of trust, a new kind of surrender, a way to be able to listen to my inner knowing.

Adyashanti encouraged me to realise that this feeling of being completely disoriented was a normal part of awakening, given that everything seemed new, and given that our perceptions had changed of ourselves and of those around us. The best insight he gave me was that the disorientation didn't arise because of the awakened mind, it arose out of the mind grasping for orientation. This was a nice concept, however, my mind was still not trained enough to avoid the grasping.

Given the extent of my pain, I finally agreed to go and see a psychiatrist. In my first session with him, he commended me on my survival strategies in life and how they were very good strategies. He noticed the sadness that came across my face, and said, "You seem sad by me saying that, why?" I finally broke down and cried with relief, saying that for so long I felt like it was my fault for bringing on my anxiety. Yes, he acknowledged, it was time to find new ways, but he saw nothing but a successful woman in front of him and questioned my need for psychiatric help. At one point, I even felt a bit rejected. I argued with him saying, "Yes, but I'm taking medication." Clearly, that meant there was something wrong with me. He could see no such relationship and told me that I seemed to have my act quite together. My meds had kicked in by the time I made it to him. I was even annoyed that I seemed so capable to him. It was as if I *wanted* to be told that there was something wrong with me. But there wasn't. I had simply driven my nervous system too hard again and failed to listen to my deeper knowing. Far too simple, it seemed, for my overly complicated, judgemental, and analytical mind.

With some Chinese herbs, more rest, less stress, and a growing community I was aligned with, I could begin to see the light at the end of the tunnel. I started to realise that no quick fix would ever do.

I needed to keep working on strengthening the core of who I really was. To allow whatever no longer resonated to simply drop away. No longer resisting. No longer denying. No longer tolerating. No longer blaming.

It was time to be still. To observe. To listen. To feel. To be. And sometimes to just be patient and trust that the answers would come.

LETTING GO

One thing that became clear to me was that I needed a part-time job that was stable so I could focus on finishing my book and the last of my jobs on the property. Through a dear friend of mine, I found a job close to home in the country working three days a week. I kept a few consulting clients and focused on my book.

A few months later, another friend encouraged me to get some volunteers to help with my property. She had been doing the same thing for a while and knew the difference they could make. I had my first volunteers lined up and ready to go, early January.

Over Christmas and the new year, I simultaneously came across a book about the power of tidying up once and for all and a documentary about the power of minimalism. With my volunteers lined up, I knew what there was to do. I was already quite tidy and minimalist, but there was a whole new level I knew I could go to. I was still feeling weighed down by my accumulated possessions, so instead of buying more shelves to store them on, I began an exercise of decluttering like never before.

This little project arose as pure inspiration. And so began the process of shedding all unnecessary possessions. No more holding onto stuff for safety. I found joy in giving them to someone who needed them, in seeing empty space open up. The more joy that emanated, the less stuff I wanted to carry. I wanted to simplify my life so I could be free to go wherever I was directed to go. Not in search of anything, rather attending to what was calling me.

I got rid of 80 percent of my books, which my friends and the library were happy to take. I got rid of half of my wardrobe with the help of friends who helped me let go of each unnecessary item. My tools now all had a place under the house. My years of filing were culled, and all I was left with was one folder. And the shipping container home my son had built was now fully functioning and no longer served as a storage room. I loved the support and the interaction with my volunteers who came from France, Germany, and New York. As my space cleared up, so did my mind.

The need to let go seemed to come all at once and in many forms. After six months of being on medication, I had the strong urge to get off them. This time around, the side effects of being on them were too much. I felt exhausted by the end of each day, and my appetite was out of control. I had put on all the weight I had lost and then some. Vanity has often been my close friend.

Two months on, around February, three synchronistic things happened. As I was working on my book, it dawned on me how many times I had said that I yearned to live in Lebanon. It had been nine years since my last return. My longest stretch yet. Then, my editor in a conversation with me said, "I have a feeling you need to go back to Lebanon." Next—and in the same week—I got an impromptu call from my older sister, who rarely calls. She said, "Sis, I feel like you have sold out on your dream of living in Lebanon."

A few months later, I followed the signs and booked my flight to Lebanon. And for the following few months, I organised my house to be put up on Airbnb to allow me to leave for an extended period of time. I found an amazing property manager who helped me put everything in place. She would manage all my bookings while I was away. I was leaving the property and my home in near perfect order and now had the right support in place, but letting go of my safe haven in the country was like pulling teeth. This kind of letting go required more of me. But still it felt like the right move. Excitement stirred.

This trip was not about escaping my life. I was simply being called back home. To my other home. For what, I had no idea. But just as I was clear about needing to write this book, I was clear about needing to face my past and reconnect with my birthplace.

My son came to visit me in the country just before I left for Lebanon. This time his reaction was different. "Look at what you have created here, Mum. I'm so proud of you." No compliment ever feels as good as a compliment I get from my son. I've lived my life wanting my parents' approval. I never realised how much parents can need their children's approval. My choices in life have often been hard for Alexander, and looking back, I can see the extent to which I failed to provide solid ground. It breaks my heart, but I also know it is never too late to heal ourselves and our children. And I am blessed with a son that is the forgiving kind.

TRANSFORMED

I am woman
I am still
I am open

Transformation comes, like death, in its own time. And like death it takes you from one dimension to another.
— Osho

Each man had only one genuine vocation—to find the way to himself... Everything else was only a would be existence, an attempt at evasion, a flight back to the ideals of the masses, conformity and fear of one's own inwardness.
— Hermann Hesse

SERENITY AND CHARISMA

Flying into Beirut, I was like a woman in love, eager to greet her lover after a long separation. My eyes were glued to the window of the plane, admiring the concrete jungle below against the beauty of the Mediterranean Sea with its stunning rock formations, Al Rouche. I will never know what draws any of us to the chaos of Lebanon. It is a clash of cultures, religions, politics, and wars. As my school friend would later tell me as I pondered my own interest in Lebanon out loud, "Lebanon has charisma." Australia gave me the stability and serenity I needed, Lebanon gave me the stirring of life I yearned for.

Since Dad's passing, Mum had returned to Lebanon. She was so excited to have me visit. Everyone she knew, knew that Cindy was arriving from Australia. Mum had arranged a taxi to pick me up from the airport. Then proceeded to call me nine times to see how close I was to arriving. Uncharacteristic behaviour on Mum's part, but I kind of liked it. She had kept my dad's car for me so I could get around, and she provided me with a stunning writing studio in the mountains overlooking Arz Jaj, which translates to the Cedars of Jaj. An idyllic setting. Now I had to resist the multiple distractions of Lebanon and focus on finishing this book. But life in Lebanon refused to be that neat and tidy. So once again I had to surrender to life and allow this book to emerge in its own timing, which it eventually did, bringing many insights with it.

GETTING COMFORTABLE WITH PAIN

All that I was learning kept bringing me back to the importance of becoming aware of my inner experience. I needed to attend to my senses. The physical sensations I felt in my body. It was not about simply observing my feelings, as some, but not all, spiritual practices suggested. I had to actually feel them. Author Marilyn Van Derbur warns that unexpressed and even repressed emotions tend to stay in the body 'like small ticking time bombs.' Bessel van der Kolk encourages 'befriending' what is going on inside of ourselves. In his book *The Body Keeps the Score* he points out that 'the rational brain cannot abolish emotions, sensations or thoughts.' He goes on to say that 'understanding why you feel a certain way does not change how you feel.'

For years, I focused on the use of personal insight to understand and transform my behaviour. However, as van der Kolk goes on to explain in his book, 'When the alarm bell of the emotional brain keeps signaling that you are in danger, no amount of insight will silence it...the centre of self-awareness has a connection with the emotional brain but the rational part of the brain does not.' The way of real healing required that I first became aware of my feelings and then to feel them at the level of body sensation. There was no other way out.

One of my biggest struggles was trying to understand why the worst of my anxiety showed up at a time in my life that felt the most stable and safe. This safe and stable part of my life, it turns out, was part of the reason my unconsciously repressed pain had the space to surface. When we feel safe in our cells, the body begins to release old emotions that have been stuck for years. This was good news, as deep cellular healing was taking place, but because of my lack of understanding, I feared and resisted the process.

On the other hand, given the unhealthy way I had been living my life in more recent years, I had reached the point where my stress cup was now overflowing, flooding my system with more chemicals than was healthy. The health of my nervous system was compromised, making it even more vulnerable to anxiety disorder.

Still, I had to learn how I could live my life differently. How I could get beyond my superwoman ways without negating all that she had offered me. And how I could remain centred while allowing my repressed pain to continue to surface and heal.

I had researched high and low for the answer. Diet, meditation, mindfulness, trauma relief, exercise, breathing, yoga, slowing down, going with the flow, and stillness. But after my crazy search to figure it all out, I finally learnt that there were no answers out there. This journey was an inward journey. I could call on all of those resources as I was guided, rather than from some deep desperation to avoid my pain.

The spiritual teachings, as well as my new learnings, kept

pointing me back to *me*. They reminded me that I had to have the courage to slow down, face my fear, feel my feelings, and dare to trust in the face of no solid ground. This journey took me deeper than I could have ever imagined possible. I had asked to go there. I just had no idea what going deeper really meant, or what it would take. Now it was just a simple matter of getting comfortable with pain.

MEDITATION: IT WILL NOT BULLET PROOF YOU FROM PAIN

Through my years of transformational work, I had mastered the ability to shift my perspective, but I was still immature when it came to acknowledging, and then staying, with my felt experience. I knew that was where my work was, but I had to dare to remain unconditionally open. I had to be constantly reminded that my job was to be with myself and my situation through all kinds of experiences. It took courage and all the strength I had at times. Along with the courage, came the compassion. Not only for me, but for all those who suffered alongside me in silence.

As my learnings deepened, I realised that my work may always be around navigating fear. Attempting to sidestep my fear only entrenched it, keeping it stuck. Slowing down and allowing it usually provided relief and, dare I say, new insight. Avoidance is often my initial reaction to my fear, but I can now catch myself more often and regain composure, accepting my feelings fully. I no longer add fear to the fear. These days, I more readily reach out for support. I still have days where I resent having to do this work. Especially when the pain runs deep.

Silence and meditation have been my antidote. But I get

arrogant as soon as I regain my power. I let go of my meditation practice, but before long, the fear returns. I go off centre and then desperately cling to my practice, hoping that it will bring comfort. I enter the practice fearing that if I don't meditate, the punishment the next day will be pain and fear. I have learnt, though, that that is not the purpose of my meditation. It is not about bullet proofing myself against pain and future suffering. So now, rather than meditating with the hope of some peaceful outcome, I am more willing to sit with whatever arises, painful or otherwise.

Some feelings can still knock me off for quite some time, be it during meditation or just in the course of my life. I actively have to muster all my strength and willingness to trust that allowing my feelings to be will eventually open me up further to the good of life. Using my head to avoid the pain, distract me from the pain, or search for the thought that may have triggered the pain, are all futile attempts to dull it, only to have the feelings resurface at some later stage.

Can I stay with myself no matter what? Yes. Sometimes. But not always. I now simply expect this to be a long process. For so long I've been trying to get rid of my pain and fear. All my strategies of avoidance were what brought me to my knees. It is my avoidance, resistance, and fear of the fear that causes it to escalate.

On a good day, I am able to feel the fear as pure sensation with no label whatsoever, and can just keep moving. On other days, I still don't allow myself to feel the pain. I tell myself that I feel this way because I have done something wrong. I didn't eat well, exercise enough, rest enough. The pain is pervasive and my mind noisy. I try to split off from the fear but just end up splitting off from myself. The way back home to myself is through the fear.

FACING MY SHAME

I also had to face the shame that kept knocking at the door. The shame of not having a job to tell people about, the shame of not knowing what I wanted to do with my life, the shame about the possibility of losing everything I had worked so hard for (if I didn't get my act together), the shame for the depth of fear, dread, and depression I had to face, the shame about the times I had to reach for medication to provide some relief when it just got too much. Avoidance was simply too painful.

I could no longer distract myself from the shame through my old driven ways. I had been pushing my shame down for years. Eventually, facing my shame did not feel like a choice. When I couldn't avoid my pain any longer, a new way cracked open. This did not mean the end of shame or fear, rather it became the beginning of something new. Life demanded to be lived in a new way.

RELINQUISHING CONTROL

I had to admit, though, that I did not know what that way was. And contrary to what I had been told for years, my job was to get out of the driver's seat and allow life to flow through me, trusting in where it was taking me.

Many a time, I fell back into the driver's seat, desperate for control. This always came at a cost: anxiety. But in those rare and precious moments where I was able to hear a deeper guidance and trust it, my life seemed to unfold in ways I could not have planned for, or imagined. Peace would return.

I am no longer exhausted and depleted, but my body demands that I stay tuned in. What worked for me yesterday may not work for me today. Trying to figure out a single way to deal with living does not work.

It is terrifying to have nowhere to go and nothing to do. It takes immense courage to allow myself to fully be in this space, but when I do, I feel complete peace. Bliss. And then it slips away. The need to control kicks in. To hold on.

Eventually, though, I learnt to follow the path I yearned for with or without fear. A path that fulfilled me now, not someday, one day. I was learning to allow it to unfold, to reveal itself in its own time, not on mine.

Living was not about trying to figure out what I wanted to

do with the rest of my life. It was about trying to figure out how I wanted to live in this moment. All we have is now. So only from here can I know where to.

But this required work. Just because I yearned for an inner-directed life, it was not going to happen overnight. Living from my centre meant—and still means—that I won't always have clear direction. Letting go happens when you are ready for it. Forcing it prematurely will only evoke more fear. So I just go where the energy takes me. I don't have to have it all figured out before I get into action. All I need to figure out is my next step. And when I don't know what that step needs to be, my job is to bring patience to the moment and trust my life will unfold when it needs to, and just the way it is supposed to. No one promised that this would be an easy path.

My biggest fear around relinquishing control has been the fear that the world will come crashing down around me. If I truly surrender control over the direction of my life, a whole new trust would be required. I feel so much peace when I truly imagine my world unfolding rather than striving, pushing, planning. When I allow my life to flow, I feel complete bliss, amazing achievement, but achievement of a different kind. Not the kind I want to brag about, but the kind that leaves me whole.

LISTENING TO LIFE

I've started to pay attention to the stir of excitement, the little flutters in my stomach, that boost of energy. It might require complete release from everything I believed before, but for now, I am paying attention. Dan Millman, in his book *Way of the Peaceful Warrior: A Book That Changes Lives,* writes, 'Everything you'll ever need to know is within you; the secrets of the universe are imprinted on the cells of your body.' So I listen to what is being communicated to me from deep within. When I slow down, trust, let go of fear, and listen, I know exactly what to do. Including doing nothing. This is not something I can force, speed up, or make happen. I tried that, too!

It has taken three years of emptying out, of terror, of reaching the limits of the dysfunction of my life, but now I can see more clearly, more often. Not always. Not every day. But more often.

When my old ways kick in, I surrender to them rather than judge or fight them. I now know the wisdom of 'All in good time.' I will let go slowly and be gentle with my journey. I allow disappointments, failures, and setbacks. They are all perfect lessons. As *A Course in Miracles* teaches: 'I don't know what anything is for.' So who am I to judge it as a disappointment, a failure, or a set back? This does not mean that I don't judge myself in that way sometimes. I have learnt not to pretend.

Life can still be hell on some days. However, now I can see the wisdom in it all. The good, the bad, and the uncomfortable.

BEING TRUE TO MYSELF

Being true to myself has not been easy. In the past, I have chosen sexy relationships over healthy relationships. Intellectual stimulation over heartfelt love. I can also see that at times, I have been the one that lacked boundaries and kindness in certain situations. The one that got needy, then bitchy. There is a grieving process in being responsible for those ways. Grief for the relationships I have lost along the way and regret for how I have left others feeling.

I can also now see how often I didn't tell the truth. Saying yes out of obligation rather than because I really wanted to say yes. Not realising that there were things that I no longer wanted to do because they didn't nourish me anymore. So I would get caught out with saying yes because I thought there must have been something wrong with me for no longer wanting to do what once gave me joy.

More and more I yearn for silence, for companionship that is based on deep resonance and the space to go deeper inside myself. This requires reducing external distractions, unnecessary drains on my energy, and tolerating what doesn't feel nourishing to my soul.

This needs to be balanced by my forgiveness work. This does not mean I invite unhealthy relationships back into my life. It does not mean tolerating or condoning what doesn't work for me. It just means not blaming anyone for my loss of peace of mind.

It also means letting go of any grievances I harbour, no matter how small they seem. I have to be both relentless about this as well as gentle. Forgiveness is not a one-time activity; it is a work in progress. And when pain hits, it is the hardest work to do. But it cannot be avoided if love and joy are my bottom line. What makes for a happy day? According to *A Course in Miracles*, 'Anything that shows up, including opportunities for forgiveness.' They say, 'Things happen for you, not to you.' A perspective I can digest more easily on a good day!

EMBRACING MY GENTLEWOMAN

My old ways of making things happen are not to be discarded lightly, though. I still love and rely on my superwoman. She is more familiar to me. She provides material safety. But I need to balance her out with my newly emerging gentlewoman. My superwoman is the container for my gentle, more sensitive, woman.

One builds the house, the other creates the home. Both are needed.

Superwoman is grounded in the physical world; gentlewoman is grounded in the spiritual world. One focuses on achievements, the other on connection with herself. I can now see that my achievements are worth nothing if I am disconnected from myself.

When my superwoman takes over, there is a cost. A cost to my health, my relationships, my peace of mind, happiness, and joy. I was so disconnected from myself, I never knew that coming home to *me* could feel so good. So peaceful, joyful, soft.

This new path, that of the gentlewoman, is less familiar. It requires that I drop down deep into my body and feel whatever is there to feel. To allow deep healing to take place. This takes time. More time than my superwoman likes. But the time it takes is worth it. And *I am worth taking the time*. The time to still myself, to nurture myself, to just be. My 'to-do' list can wait. I am always a better me when I take this time.

My superwoman often lacks trust in me, in others, and in the world. She has low tolerance for uncertainty and seeks safety from life and relationships. My gentlewoman may, at times, disappoint others, but she never disappoints herself. She has nowhere to get to but now. She trusts life to provide all the openings she needs. And she knows that joy is sourced from simplicity, stillness, and love rather than doing.

My superwoman was born out of 'something going wrong.' For her, life is hard and unsafe, but she makes things happen no matter what. It is my gentlewoman that will help her heal so she can accomplish, because she is passionate rather than broken.

As I loosen the grip of my old superwoman ways, a space opens up. One that is unfamiliar. Uncertain. One that can cause anxiety, given I no longer have the old behavioural or emotional patterns to hold onto. But in this space, there is room for new ways to emerge from within. New ways that are informed by my past experiences but not limited by, or to, them.

In the absence of gentlewoman, superwoman gets trapped by trying to fix the world, avoiding fear, and ensuring safety and security. Gentlewoman heals the world by healing herself first, undoing perceptions of fear, lack, and uncertainty.

Superwoman's outer life often looks fabulous, but not always. She can be the envy of many others. Some may even be in awe of her. However, her inner life is often out of control with no one ever knowing.

Gentlewoman knows deep down that her power arises when she has no need for 'something to be done.' It does not mean she has no needs, it just means that nothing must be done outside of herself, or by another, in order for her to be at peace.

Gentlewoman is a space you come from. A space that cannot always be defined in words. When we surrender to our gentlewoman, we are willing to put our intellect, knowledge, and expectations aside and truly give ourselves to the moment. To life. Gentlewoman is not a place to get to; it is about letting go and allowing what already is. Gentlewoman emanates from stillness and silence. It is the part of us that is hidden from us but has always been there quietly waiting to be awakened.

Superwoman may have been born to survive my life's disappointments and to help me cope with the stress of this so-called modern world. But superwoman also yearns to turn inward in search of spiritual fulfilment. She has outgrown her love of worldly ambition. Just like yin and yang need each other to form the whole, superwoman and gentlewoman complement each other, making each other whole.

It takes time to learn gentlewoman's natural flow. She refuses to be told how to live her life. She wants to be *sourced* by life. Embracing her may require full surrender, but she also imbues me with new strength.

IT WILL ALWAYS BE A WORK IN PROGRESS

As I come out from the darkness, I have a newfound respect for my superwoman. She serves me. She protects me. She is there when I need her. She is courageous, but she cannot be taken advantage of. She can be wild, yet wonderful. She can be the life of the party or the holder of space. She is multi-faceted, deep, wise, unwilling to ever give up.

I have missed her. She is no longer who I am, but a *part* of who I am.

My superwoman is now tempered by my gentlewoman. My gentlewoman offers clear direction, but first she demands that I listen to her cues. And if I don't listen, she will not speak. My gentlewoman would never dishonour me that way. She emerges out of stillness and waits for me to choose her ways. Integrating both my superwoman and my gentlewoman has been the access to being a whole woman. We often have glimpses of who we really are, but it is quite a journey to fully own who we are. And it will always be a work in progress.

There is something so profound and powerful when I have those rare moments of experiencing being a whole woman. I am able to remain still no matter how crazy the world seems on the outside. I remain at the centre of the storm. I am clear. I can't be rattled by anyone. But there is no formula. There are no steps. Those moments come when I authentically let go of how I think my life should be, when I dare to listen to the voice that leads me to pure joy. I know it is possible, because I have been there. I want it to be my path. My path to right here. My path to right now.

> *I said to my soul, be still and wait without hope,*
> *For hope would be hope for the wrong thing; wait without love,*
> *For love would be love of the wrong thing; there is yet faith,*
> *But the faith and the love and the hope are all in the waiting.*
> *Wait without thought, for you are not ready for thought;*
> *So the darkness shall be the light, and the stillness the dancing.*
> — T.S. Eliot

RESOURCES

BOOKS

These books were a lifeline in my time of need:
    Claire Weekes, *Hope and Help for Your Nerves (audiobook)*
    Joseph Jaworski, *Synchronicity: The Inner Path of Leadership*
    Paul Foxman, *Dancing with Fear*
    Bessel van der Kolk, *The Body Keeps the Score*
    Dr. Helen Schucman, *A Course in Miracles*

WEBSITES

One of the best online resources for anxiety sufferers:
    The Anxiety Center, *anxietycentre.com*

SPIRITUAL TEACHERS

My favorite spiritual teachers who taught me and kept reminding me to be with my fear:

Adyashanti, *adyashanti.org*
Pema Chodron, *pemachodronfoundation.org*
Alan Watts, *alanwatts.org*
Marianne Williamson, *marianne.com*
Eckhart Tolle, *eckharttolle.com*

TRAUMA EXPERTS

Towards the end of writing my book, I discovered these wonderful teachers who shed light on trauma, childhood development, and addiction, as well as healing at the body level:

Gabor Mate, *drgabormate.com*
Irene Lyons, *irenelyon.com*
Peter Levine, *psychotherapy.net/interview/interview-peter-levine*

TRAUMA RESEARCH

A study anyone suffering from a mental health condition should know about:
The Adverse Childhood Experiences Study, *acestudy.org*

SPECIAL THANKS

Just as I was coming back to life after my first bout of anxiety disorder, I attended a one-day writing workshop with Catherine Deveny. Catherine, who took my book idea seriously, later became my writing mentor, allowing me to relate to myself as a writer. Her support was my launching ground.

Deep gratitude goes to my editors Jen Keehn and Angie Frazier, without whom this book would not have come to fruition. The months spent patiently revising, reshaping, and attending to every minor detail was invaluable. Without their trust in my vision for the book, it would not have become a reality.

Special thanks go to my son and my mother. My son, for always believing in my book, especially during times of doubt and fear around exposing my personal story, which also included him. In those times, he reminded me of the purpose of this book, saying that if at least one person got something out of it, it would be a success. And my mother, for trusting me to write about our family events with the grace and cultural sensitively that was required, never interfering with the content.

Along the way, support came from many directions, each deserving special thanks:

My brother and my sister-in-law, who housed and fed me during my hardest days. My older sister would spontaneously call, reminding me of anecdotes from our childhood and allowing humour to enter the heavy topic of anxiety. My younger sister, the creative one of the family, adjudicated on what was to stay and what had to go in the final version. My dear friends Corinne Noyes, Elizabeth Reinoga, Jenny Mohn, and Sonia Stocco and their families, all of whom provided ongoing support as well as their homes as safe havens during my healing.

To all the people who read the evolving manuscript, offered advice, and provided the cheerleading I needed along the way, your insight has made a great difference: Melanie Altas, Rabih Andraos, Renee Andary, Martine Btaich, Meg Corson, Leah Davidson, Carolyn Dean, Charles Duff, Neil Gibb, Barb Hodgens, Lena Mitchell, Nada Mtanios, Dunia Daou, Emma Newnes, Marg Peck, Julie Postance, Nadine Sassine, Sabine Sassine, Merle Singer, Amanda Siviter, Ana Stankovski, and Lina Yeo-Blake.

To the late Claire Weekes whose books and wisdom first opened the door of hope, and whose work inspired and sustained me.

And, if it is even possible, I'd like to thank the process of writing this book. There were many days where it was my only respite. It was my way out of the silent darkness that pervaded my world.

Much has changed since then, and will continue to change,

and I thank everyone who has played a part in my evolution. Through this book I want fellow anxiety sufferers to know that they are not alone, they are not weak, they have nothing to be ashamed of, and that healing is possible. But it will always be a work in progress.

www.ingramcontent.com/pod-product-compliance
Lightning Source LLC
Chambersburg PA
CBHW032024290426
44110CB00012B/665